MW00928706

Praise for
Unleashing Your Courageous Compassion

Unleashing Your Courageous Compassion is an important book that comes at an important time.

It has become more critical than ever for Christians to lead the way, not only saving the lives of the unborn but also ensuring that they have abundant lives. *Unleashing Your Courageous Compassion* reminds us why this work is central to God's kingdom and how we can, humbly and prayerfully, do our part in it.

—Roland C. Warren, *President and CEO of Care Net*

Far from the spotlight, many compassionate souls reach out in love, through faith, with hope. These champions are on the front lines of life-and-death decisions, and they need to be refreshed and encouraged regularly. Others have resisted the call and need to know that they can, and will, be anointed for the challenge. Susanne masterfully conveys the undergirding truths necessary for all who would champion the gift of life and the Giver of life.

—Jor-El Godsey, *President, Heartbeat International*

Refreshment, challenge, and inspiration all will come from reading this powerful devotional. Those who have worked long years to restore the sanctity of human life in our nation need to read and meditate upon the wonderful insights that Susanne Maynes provides in this wonderful work. Thanks, Susanne, for this gift to us.

—Thomas A. Glessner, *JD, President,*
National Institute of Family and Life Advocates (NIFLA)

With a fresh, provocative style, Susanne takes the reader on a 40-day journey bent on awakening and restoring a passion for life-affirming service of the Giver of all life. Whether you are brand-new to the battle for life, or you have been involved in this labor of love for over 40 years as I have, this engaging book will lead you deep into God's heart for his children—both born and unborn.

—*Margaret H. Hartshorn, PhD, Founder and former President, Heartbeat International, Inc.*

Susanne has gathered together Scripture, testimonies, and beautiful words of poetry to provide us with an empowering devotional for all believers. *Unleashing Your Courageous Compassion* offers the hope and encouragement so many of us need to trust God as he leads us to serve in his kingdom and to keep trusting and abiding in him through the challenges and victories of life ministry.

—*Melinda Delahoyde, Vice-President, Life International and former President, Care Net*

How do I stay devoted to the cause of life? In part, by reading devotionally. Take 40 days to read *Unleashing Your Courageous Compassion*, and you'll share with me a burning heart to stand for life with courage and compassion.

—*John Ensor, President, PassionLife, Author of **Answering the Call***

Prior to ascending to our Father in heaven, Jesus did not foster passivity amongst the ranks of his chosen apostles, but charged them to make disciples of all nations. *Unleashing Your Courageous Compassion*: 40 Reflections on Rescuing the Unborn spurs the reader to become a staunch defender of life, by elucidating a visceral understanding of today's pro-death culture. My hope is that everyone will read this work and be inspired to respond to our Lord's great commission to defend the lives of his future disciples.

—*Fr. Frank Pavone, National Director, Priests for Life President, National Pro-Life Religious Council*

Susanne has created a gift to those who serve with courageous compassion the women, children, and families in thousands of pregnancy care facilities around the United States, Canada, and the world. Whether the 30-year veteran executive director or a new volunteer of a life-affirming ministry, all can come to the river and drink deep the waters of life. What a marvelous 40-day journey of encouragement, challenge, and truth to feed the mind and soul.

—John C. Cissel II, SIOR, Former Board Chairman,
Heartbeat International, President, Visioneering Real Estate Inc.

Unleashing Your Courageous Compassion is a dynamic devotional for those who seek a gentle current to travel the waters of grief and loss. Each section offers a down-to-earth, approachable perspective, encouraging the reader to dive further into the devotions. Susanne provides readers with a creative opportunity to be active in prayer coupled with self-reflection for life-changing promises and inspiration.

—Theresa Burke, PhD, Founder, Rachel's Vineyard Ministries, Author
of **Forbidden Grief: The Unspoken Pain of Abortion**

I found a new recruitment tool. *Unleashing Your Courageous Compassion* is a thunderous and action-inspiring call to the church to get off the pew and get into the culture. I have been serving in culture of life ministries for over twenty-five years, and these thought-provoking devotions challenged my commitment to the cause. For those who have been on the sidelines, Susanne gives a passionate call to be champions for the cause of life. Let the volunteer army begin!

—Patrick Eades, Executive Director of
Care Net Pregnancy Center of Coastal Georgia

Unleashing Your Courageous Compassion will bring you into a safe place of answering the call to pregnancy center work. All the fears, doubts, and anxieties are addressed in a gentle, encouraging, biblical way. I highly recommend it as a devotional for pregnancy centers with new volunteers and volunteers who want to grow in their service.

—Linda Cochrane, RN, CEO, Hopeline Pregnancy Resource Center, Author of Forgiven and Set Free

Susanne gives us a compelling reminder that the follower of Christ, while saved by grace and not by works, has been saved for a purpose. That purpose is service that is valuable to the kingdom. "For we are his workmanship, created in Christ Jesus for good works, which God prepared beforehand, that we should walk in them" (Ephesians 2:10 ESV). The work to which God has called us may appear at times to be a burden, but Susanne reminds us that there is a special joy in embracing the burden.

—Tom Mason, Former Executive Vice-President, Focus on the Family, Care Net Board Member

Susanne has written an amazing daily devotional that will powerfully motivate, challenge, and help equip men and women to look at how much God, our creator, values the sanctity of life and the miracles being manifested each day through the life-affirming ministries that he has raised up for such a time as this. Susanne's insights and descriptions of our human condition will help the reader seek spiritual growth and strength that can only come from a deep, daily, determined, and intentional relationship with Jesus Christ. Be prepared to be deeply and profoundly moved and challenged to grow in your faith, more fully understand the power of the Holy Spirit, and to seek God's perfect will as to how you can make an eternal impact concerning the sanctity of life in helping transform our nation back to a culture of life.

—Sol Pitchon, CEO and President of the New Life Solutions Family of Ministries

unleashing your courageous compassion

40 REFLECTIONS ON RESCUING THE UNBORN

Susanne Maynes

Unless otherwise indicated, all Scriptures are from The Holy Bible, English Standard Version® (ESV®), copyright © 2001 by Crossway, a publishing ministry of Good News Publishers. Used by permission. All rights reserved.

Scripture quotations marked (NIV) are from the Holy Bible, New International Version® NIV® Copyright © 1973, 1978, 1984, 2011 by Biblica, Inc.® Used by permission. All rights reserved worldwide.

This book is dedicated to my husband Scott; my partner in ministry, my best friend, and my beloved for life. You are a man of excellent spirit. I'm so grateful to the Lord Jesus for taking us on this adventure together.

*The stories told in these pages are true stories
of people I've had the privilege of serving.
All names have been changed
to protect client confidentiality.*

Table of Contents

Welcome to the Water

I guess you could call me a church lady. Most ministries I've been involved in have taken place exclusively in the context of my local congregation. A few years ago, I reached a point of frustration. I didn't see much fruit from my efforts, and I longed to touch my community more effectively.

I decided to volunteer at a pregnancy resource center (PRC), thinking I'd talk to middle-class girls who had made a mistake on prom night. Quickly, my understanding of the issues surrounding abortion—and about our culture as a whole—radically changed.

If I were nineteen today, my worldview would likely be completely different. Sexual activity with multiple partners would seem normal to me. My definition of sexual responsibility would be the proper use of birth control. I'd rationalize that it's fine to live together before marriage, even as a churchgoer. And if someone asked about my stance on abortion, I'd probably say, "I wouldn't choose abortion personally, but I'd never judge someone who did."

Reaching out to those facing unplanned pregnancies in my community has changed me. Before I got involved in ministry outside of the church, I was ignorant of many cultural trends. The struggles faced by young Christians and non-Christians were a mystery to me. Now I actually get it.

Maybe you're a church lady or church guy too. This book will fortify your understanding of the sanctity of human life and help you understand the rapidly changing society we live in.

I invite you to join me at the edge of a river.

In Ezekiel 47, the prophet followed the command to enter the waters flowing from God's temple, but he didn't dive in. He walked into ankle-deep water, then thigh-deep, and finally got waist-deep before the river was too deep for wading.

On a summer camping trip one year, my husband and I crossed the swiftly flowing Salmon River on foot. That is, he crossed the river. When I reached the deepest part, I panicked and turned around.

Fear of being swept away kept me from venturing into new territory.

God's gentle but irresistible pull to go deeper with him is like walking into a river. As we surrender to serve him more intentionally, we may feel anxious at first—but we don't want to miss what's on the opposite side.

Will you walk with me into the river of God? Will you offer Jesus this next season of your life and allow him to transform you? You may feel challenged and stretched as we explore some uncharted waters together. But at the end of this journey, you'll feel refreshed and empowered.

Let the river wash away the old life of doubt, fear, and disappointment. Get baptized into a new life of courageous compassion.

It's time to get wet.

PART ONE:
The Call

"And Jesus said to them, 'Follow me,
and I will make you become fishers of men.'
And immediately they left their nets
and followed him."
—Mark 1:17-18

TAPESTRY

Stretched taut between
circumstance and destiny,
the fabric of
my life lies pressed
in two dimensions

Suddenly,
the white-hot needle of
I Am
plummets through eternity and
pierces stubborn cloth

Breathless and undone,
I bear the fresh mark
He leaves behind

One more stitch
toward glory

Previously published in **The Salvation Army War Cry**, *back cover, August 2, 2003.*

An Expectant Heart

When Jesus walked the dusty roads of Palestine, he often interrupted people. He called Simon and Andrew as they set sail for a day's work *(Mark 1:16-18)*. He summoned Matthew when he was busy collecting taxes *(Matthew 9:9)*.

Jesus still interrupts people. You're minding your own business, occupied with the routines of life, when he shows up and turns things upside-down.

Maybe you receive a newsletter in the mail, get invited to a fundraiser, or hear a speaker on the radio. You've heard the life-affirming mission being promoted before, but this time the appeal stays on your mind. You can't ignore it any longer.

Giving financially is important, but you can't shake the sense that there's more to this conviction. God is asking you to drop what you're doing to make this ministry a priority. You may not quit your job to do so, but every yes requires a corresponding no. To say yes to the Master's call will mean saying no to something else.

Americans are busy. We're proud of our busyness and even hide behind it. But activity doesn't equal purposeful living. At some point, between working, playing, and attending church meetings, we need to awaken to the reality, *I was made for more than this.*

All Simon and Andrew had ever known was fishing. How could they drop their livelihood—their identity—to roam the countryside, following an itinerant rabbi?

They had expectant hearts.

These brothers, like all Jews of their time, were waiting for the long-hoped-for Messiah. But they didn't wait passively. They listened to the preaching of John the Baptist, whose message was repentance. They even encountered Jesus personally right after John identified him as the Lamb of God.

Perhaps Andrew and Simon didn't fully understand what it would be like to follow the Messiah once they found him. But they were ready and willing. They left behind their nets to go with Jesus—without hesitation, without question.

Has the Lamb of God encountered you and found an expectant heart? Do you know you were made for more than the ordinary tasks of living?

Allow Jesus to interrupt you. Allow him to pierce you with what pierces him. He wants to take you on an adventure.

*"For my thoughts are not your thoughts, neither are your ways my ways,' declares the Lord." —**Isaiah 55:8***

Going Deeper

Before you go to sleep tonight, review your day. Think about the agenda you had—what you hoped to accomplish, what pressed on your mind, encounters you had with people. Then ask Jesus one simple question and record his answer: *Lord Jesus, what mattered to you today?*

_____

_____

_____

_____

_____

_____

_____

_____

_____

_____

_____

_____

UNLIKELY HERO

I am Bilbo Baggins of Bag-End. I like
my books, my garden, my favorite
chair. I do not want an adventure;
they seem quite dangerous, and I don't
need the excitement, thank you.

I like going to church. I sing in the choir
and go to Bible study and co-lead
a weekly small group. I even give
to the poor. I'm quite busy and content
right here in the shire.

Besides, I'm not very brave. I don't know
one end of a sword from the other. I need
three square meals and a warm bed. I'm
not much of a burglar at all, really. Surely
you don't want me to come along?

Whose Adequacy Is It, Anyway?

As creatures with a default mode of self-focus, it's easy for us to take stock of our weaknesses and inadequacies before we commit to a task. Like Bilbo Baggins in J.R.R. Tolkien's *The Hobbit*, we don't want to look foolish or feel like a failure, so we try to bow out beforehand.

Consider Moses, who led a multitude of Hebrew slaves out of captivity and guided them through a hostile wilderness—across a sea, no less—to a homeland of their own. God worked stunning miracles through Moses' hands and voice. He was one of Israel's greatest leaders.

Yet at first, Moses didn't believe he could say a word to Pharaoh *(see Exodus 3 and 4)*. "I can't speak before Pharaoh, mighty ruler of all Egypt. L-l-l-lord, you know I don't t-t-t-talk so good!"

Maybe you have a Moses mind-set.

"I could never coach girls making a pregnancy decision, or help someone with addictions, or talk to a homeless stranger. Lord, you know that's too scary for me!"

Our excuses, hesitations, and rationalizations before God have repeated themselves many times in human history. But here's the thing … God isn't calling you to co-labor with him because he thinks you're up for the task.

He's calling you precisely because you aren't.

When God accomplishes his purposes in the earth, he chooses to do so through weak human vessels. He created us. He doesn't need our strength or abilities. Rather, he wants to let *his* strength flow through us as we learn to depend on him.

The point is not ability, but availability.

Moses' response angered God, but he graciously allowed Moses to take his brother Aaron along as a mouthpiece. God isn't impressed when we respond to his call with excuses instead of obedience. When we make choices about ministry based on our inadequacy, we're telling God that we refuse to trust him.

When Moses balked, did he allow for almighty God to move through his flawed servant, to work on behalf of his people and make his glory known? In the same way, when we make excuses, we fail to take into account all God wants to do for us and through us.

Thankfully, the Lord is long-suffering and kind. He used Moses mightily despite his resistance. He wants to use you too.

Don't fret about your inadequacies; rather, rejoice in *his* adequacy.

"But he said to me, 'My grace is sufficient for you, for my power is made perfect in weakness.' Therefore I will boast all the more gladly of my weaknesses, so that the power of Christ may rest upon me."
—2 Corinthians 12:9

Going Deeper

When it comes to ministry, what personal weaknesses tempt you to say "I can't"? Write them down. Then thank God for working through your weaknesses to make his glory known.

_____

_____

_____

_____

_____

_____

_____

_____

_____

_____

_____

A GREATER FIRE

There burns within my soul a greater fire
than striving for the highest earthly goal;
to be the King's bondslave is my desire.

I would not after worldly dreams aspire,
to chase a dream, or play an empty role;
there burns within my soul a greater fire.

I seek to do God's will, and never tire
of doing right, no matter what the toll;
to be the King's bondslave is my desire.

I do not seek rewards which men admire,
The riches, fame and pleasure they extol;
there burns within my heart a greater fire.

It is a narrow road that takes me higher,
transcending earth, enrapturing my soul;
to be the King's bondslave is my desire.

I care not that a great price is required;
the world's playthings can never make me whole.
There burns within my soul a greater fire;
to be the King's bondslave is my desire.

Counting the Cost

If anyone had reason for hesitating to do God's will, it was Mary. She became pregnant out of wedlock in a time and culture where she stood to lose everything—her reputation, her fiancé, even her life.

The angel Gabriel's announcement didn't exactly invite Mary into a life of ease or glamour. Despite her youth, however, she was a woman of faith and courage. She no doubt sensed what was on the line when she uttered the words, "Let it be to me according to your word" *(Luke 1:38)*. She knew that her yes could lead to rejection and pain, yet she believed these sacrifices would be worth it for the honor of participating in God's great plan of salvation for all mankind.

Mary is more than a great model for young women who face an unplanned pregnancy; she's an example for any of us when we receive an assignment from God and are frightened by what following him might cost us. We anxiously lay down our precious pennies, not realizing we're purchasing the pearl of great price.

Serving Jesus is often costly.

But do you really value things that come easily, with a cheap price tag?

The good news about serving God is that every bit of investment will yield multiplied returns. It may feel like a gamble, and you may not see the reward right away, but it will surely be worth any temporal loss you might experience in the exchange.

Vindication may take time too. We need eyes to see and ears to hear so we can rejoice when God whispers his pleasure in our obedience.

I learned that principle while homeschooling our three sons. For fourteen years, I regularly battled self-doubt and questioned my abilities, living out a choice many in our culture find foolish. One of our sons eventually earned his degree in English/secondary education. At a reception honoring scholarship recipients, the head of the education department took me aside and thanked me for the job I had done with home education.

It took years of effort before I heard the words that vindicated my struggle, but it was well worth my investment. That evening, I wrote about that sweet reward in my journal, thanking God for the way he let me participate in his plan for my sons.

As you hear God calling you right now, may I encourage you to step out in faith? It's worth all the time, energy, and finances to experience the favor and pleasure of God.

Choose to say, as Mary did, "Let it be to me according to your word." And one day, you'll hear him say, "Well done, good and faithful servant" *(Matthew 25:21)*.

"If anyone comes to me [Jesus] and does not hate his own father and mother and wife and children and brothers and sisters, yes, and even his own life, he cannot be my disciple. Whoever does not bear his own cross and come after me cannot be my disciple." —**Luke 14:26-27**

Going Deeper

What might it cost you to invest yourself in life-affirming ministry? Do you have concerns about giving up valuable time, taking a stand on a politicized issue, or giving finances sacrificially? Let God search your heart for a few minutes.

Lord Jesus, as I commit myself to follow you wherever you lead, I release these specific concerns to you today:

_____

_____

_____

_____

_____

_____

_____

_____

_____

THE WORSHIPER

She slips another dirty dish into
soap-bubbled water, swiping off
smudges of peanut butter and grape
jelly, rinsing under gushing warmth,
singing, **Bless the Lord, oh my soul,**
Oh, my soul, worship his holy name;
Sing like never before, oh my soul,
Worship his holy name, *clatter of*
plates accompanying praise, music
ascending to heaven, sweetest offering;
descending to hell, holy terror shaking
foundations, crumbling strongholds,
sending shrieking demons running.

She dries and stacks and wonders
if she'll always just be ordinary.

Let's Look at Your Resumé

I could never talk to people who are facing unplanned pregnancies because…

I'm shy and inexperienced.

I'm not familiar with social work.

I can't relate to their lifestyle.

I'm not a Bible expert.

I'm not a licensed therapist.

I'm not trained in sonography.

There are many reasons to feel disqualified from something God asks us to do. However, God doesn't choose people the way a typical employer selects them. He chooses us more for our weaknesses than for our strengths, so his glory can be made evident.

On the other hand, it's also true that God equips those he calls. Many times we aren't aware of how he has been preparing us all along until we obey.

Have you ever taken a look at your spiritual resumé?
You might be shocked at how much is already on it.

Have you helped a friend through a hard emotional season? Have you read and studied the Bible and listened to sermons? Have you raised children? Have you served in any kind of ministry at church?

Can you read and write at a high-school level? Have you been married for a few years? Do you know how to clean house, pay bills, dress for a job interview? Can you make a grocery list and cook nutritious meals?

Do you know some effective ways to handle stress? Is prayer part of your routine? Do you have hope, joy, and peace in your life because of Jesus?

If you possess any of the above qualifications, you have something to offer a young man trapped in generational poverty, or a young couple trying to get along with each other, or a teen girl facing a pregnancy decision.

You may still wonder, *Don't I need specialized skills to volunteer at a pregnancy center?* Your local pregnancy center provides topnotch training for pregnancy-options coaching and life-skills mentoring. In addition, many centers offer training in sonography for nurses—a critical part of this lifesaving ministry.

Here's the thing: you have life experience. You have skills other people have not been able to learn. You have stability, and you have godly wisdom to offer. On top of all that, you'll receive thorough, practical training, which you'll find helpful anywhere you serve in ministry.

So, that resumé of yours?

It shows you are qualified.

"And so, from the day we heard, we have not ceased to pray for you, … giving thanks to the Father, who has qualified you to share in the inheritance of the saints in light." —Colossians 1:9,12

Going Deeper

Write down your spiritual qualifications and life experience as if you were preparing an employment resumé. Don't skip anything, assuming it doesn't count. Use a separate sheet if necessary. Ask the Lord to remind you of accomplishments you may have forgotten. You'll be encouraged—and you'll be ready to accept the specific ministry "job" he has for you.

_____

_____

_____

_____

_____

_____

_____

_____

_____

_____

_____

COMPASSION

Your mercy will not snuff a smoldering wick,
but cups a hand around the faltering spark;
as you breathe life into the candlestick,
hope leaps to flame once more against the dark.

Your mercy will not break a drooping reed,
but gently holds upright the crippled stem
and touches it with soothing balm to heal;
then binds it to your strength to stand again.

Your mercy is the whispering of my name;
a still, small voice, the murmuring of a dove
that silences the haunting power of shame;
such is the power of your unfailing love.

Your mercy is my spirit's grateful song
that I will sing to you my whole life long.

*Previously published in **The Salvation Army War Cry**, May 2003, n.p*

Wounded Healers

I know a woman who desires to serve God. She cares about people and wants to minister to others, but she hesitates to do so.

She doesn't feel ready.

You see, as a young girl, this woman was sexually abused. She still deals with chronic insomnia and migraines, and she has trouble relating to her husband sexually. So she promises herself, *When I get healed, then I'll minister to others.*

Maybe you've been through a similar anguish. Or maybe you've been wounded by a divorce, bound by physical limitations, or saddled with a load of debt. Maybe you've told yourself the same thing: *Once I'm over this, I can reach out to others.*

Yes, we're less distracted once God has helped us resolve our major issues. But each of us is also a work in progress. We won't see the end result of what we'll be until we stand with Christ in glory.

Following Jesus is no guarantee of a pain-free life; in fact, he promised us trouble in this world *(John 16:33)*. Until all things are made new and our righteous Judge rules in the age to come, we'll suffer. We'll have to choose forgiveness or bitterness, believing or doubting, generosity or stinginess. We'll also have opportunities to reach out to others while we're still mending.

Ministering despite personal brokenness requires trust. God deserves our yes even while we have unfinished business in our soul and body.

As we step out in faith to answer his call, he'll repair us along the way.

In John chapter 5, Jesus asks the man at the pool of Bethesda if he wants to be healed. Instead of answering the question, the sick man goes into a lengthy explanation of why he hasn't been healed.

The man has a singular notion of how healing must take place, and it has much to do with his own effort. From his perspective, there's only one window of opportunity—get into the pool first when the waters move.

All this man seeks is the chance to explain his embarrassing predicament and get a little sympathy. He has pretty much lost hope for getting his life back. Yet think of it—he recites this diagnosis, this problem, to Jesus. Jesus, by whom and for whom all things were created. Jesus, who has the power to heal all disease.

Jesus listens, ready to reverse thirty-eight years of infirmity with a word.

He's still listening today. He listens to you—the laments, the limitations, the reasons you can't serve him yet. He's ready to change it all.

You can look to yourself and others for answers. You can recite reasons the healing hasn't happened yet. You can aim for sympathy as your highest hope.

Or you can trust and obey Jesus—and find healing on the way.

*"Here is my servant, whom I uphold, my chosen one in whom I delight. ...
He will not shout or cry out, or raise his voice in the streets. A bruised reed he
will not break, and a smoldering wick he will not snuff out."*
—Isaiah 42:1-3 (NIV)

Going Deeper

In what ways do you feel like a bruised reed or a smoldering wick?
Have you been hoping for sympathy rather than asking for healing? Set
aside some time to listen to Jesus. Allow him to breathe on you and bind
you up.

_____

_____

_____

_____

_____

_____

_____

_____

_____

_____

_____

THE SHAPING

I am wet clay slapped onto
potter's stone wheel, spinning,
squeezed between thumb
and fingertips,
spinning,
pressed by hands molding,
relentless, careful caress,
always the spinning,
the pushing
as he fashions what
he will. He puts me in fire
to harden, then glaze.
I emerge, a fit
and shining vessel.

God's Masterpiece

Each devotional in this book has been paired with a poem, a work of art crafted with words. Did you know that you are a work of art too?

Ephesians 2:10 says, "For we are his workmanship, created in Christ Jesus for good works which God prepared beforehand, that we should walk in them." The Greek word for workmanship is *poema,* from which we get the English word poem. So God is the poet, and you are his *poem,* his work in progress.

Not only is he working on you, but he's also working *in and through you.* This Scripture makes clear that our sovereign God has actually created opportunities for you to do specific good works in your lifetime. And he planned them before the earth was formed.

Let that sink in.

The neighbor to whom you are supposed to lend a hand? Planned before the earth began to spin in space. Those meals you were meant to provide for the local food bank? Designed before God put fish in the ocean. That scared pregnant girl you were meant to reach with your kindness and listening ear? Ordained before dirt existed.

Just like the description in Jeremiah 18, God is the potter, and you are the clay.

The universe is far from random and meaningless, as humanists would have us believe. A sovereign God has planned your steps, and he has more ahead for you than you can think to ask or imagine.

But a voice in your head keeps you from believing your obedience matters. You hear whispers: *You aren't up for the task. It's too hard. You're nothing.*

One of Satan's most effective tactics is discouragement. When we start walking in the purposes of God, Satan attacks quickly, attempting to dissuade us before we get going.

He's afraid of what you can accomplish.

Satan's goal is to lie, steal, kill, and destroy *(John 10:10)*. God's goal is to redeem, restore, and resurrect. As you obey God, you'll prevent the enemy from carrying out his sinister plans in your life and in other people's lives. You'll be an emissary of truth, light, and hope—an ambassador of the gospel.

You, God's masterpiece, will partner with God as he works on many masterpieces through your hands. That's how it works.

Never mind the ceiling of the Sistine Chapel, the *Mona Lisa,* or *Hamlet.* An artist greater than Michelangelo, Da Vinci, or Shakespeare is at work. And the masterpiece is you.

God says, *"Behold, like the clay in the potter's hand, so are you in my hand."*
—Jeremiah 18:6

Going Deeper

Describe a time when God set up a specific opportunity for you to serve someone in Jesus's name. How did this encounter change you?

_____

_____

_____

_____

_____

_____

_____

_____

_____

_____

_____

_____

_____

FROM THE LOW PLACE RAISED

I

Heat presses down like a weight on the wide
valley, littered for miles with bare white
bones. Whirlwinds spin, throwing dust upwards
off what remains of
my dreams

Here was sinew and tendon, muscle and
organ, marrow and cartilage. Here was
a blood-pulsing horde of warriors running,
shouting, lunging, living river
flowing forward

now stripped and scattered,
turning to earth

   Why would you bring me here to witness this
   dry sea of death? I dare not answer
   your question

   Human child, can these bones live?

FROM THE LOW PLACE RAISED (cont.)

II

Be my oracle. Give them
My message

> *I muster puny, faltering faith*
> *to speak your words over*
> *hope's graveyard*

> > *Oh, dry bones, hear this. You will*
> > *no longer languish in decay. I will*
> > *breathe into you, cover you with sinew*
> > *and muscle and skin. You will*
> > *live again and you will know who*
> > *I Am*

> *I hear rustling, rattling, clicking like sticks, a great*
> *clattering across the plain. Skull to spine,*
> *femur to phalanges, skeletons form*

> > *I watch as flesh and skin*
> > *clothe bone, a countless army*
> > *reassembled. They lay where slain,*
> > *still, unbreathing*

FROM THE LOW PLACE RAISED <small>(cont.)</small>

III

Summon my Spirit. Invite the Breath
to return

   I fill my lungs and cry out

      Come, Spirit. Come from the four winds and
      breathe on these. Resurrect what has been
      long dead. Make all things new. Come!

   Movement ripples across the plain. Heads
   rise, knees draw toward chests, arms push torsos
   upward, feet plant themselves on the ground.
   Thousands stand, row upon row, a living army,
   eyes fixed forward

      I am the Power that opens graves,
      the Author of your future. Know me,
      take hope, and
      live

Resurrecting Your Dreams

Deep down, a hunger rumbles in you to make a difference during your days on earth. You have gifts. You have dreams. You long to see them fulfilled.

Perhaps you ardently pursued your God-dream for a while. You saw it taking shape. Then something happened. Maybe it was traumatic; maybe you can't even put your finger on it.

Either way, your dream died.

Sometimes we give up on a dream because it seems too insignificant or too difficult, or we lack guidance and encouragement. The opposition is too fierce. Distractions pull us away. Time passes, and we find ourselves distanced from our passion, trapped by circumstances and not sure how we were ensnared.

So we trudge on, doing what lies in front of us. But the graveyard of our God-dream haunts us. In unguarded moments, we feel sad, grieving the death of that dream, wondering if it is yet possible.

There is every reason to hope. God is in the resurrection business. And resurrection always opens new dimensions. When Jesus appeared to his disciples after he was raised from the dead, he ate fish with them, yet he could walk through walls.

The same, only better. That's what resurrection looks like.

Jesus said, "'Truly, truly, I say to you, unless a grain of wheat falls into the earth and dies, it remains alone; but if it dies, it bears much fruit'" *(John 12:24)*. God is sovereign. He allows dreams in our heart to die because he intends to bring them back better than ever, bearing much fruit for the glory of his name.

What dreams have you cherished in your heart? Do you love to come alongside hurting people and minister mercy to them? Do you have a passion for teaching homemaking skills to young women? Do you long to help young men become excellent fathers? Do you want to see children growing up in emotionally healthy homes, free from abuse and neglect?

Be honest with yourself. No matter how small, how impossible, how crazy—in what way do you desire to partner with God?

Now is the time for your dreams to be resurrected. Now is the time for you to find your place in God's kingdom by serving in the way he designed you to serve.

Now is the time for your dead bones to come back to life.

"Then he said to me, 'Prophesy over these bones, and say to them, "O dry bones, hear the word of the Lord."'" **—Ezekiel 37:4**

Going Deeper

Read all of Ezekiel 37 with your senses tuned to the scene before the prophet. Talk to God aloud about the dead places in your heart, the visions you still long to see fulfilled. Commit your dreams afresh to him and trust him to resurrect them.

_____

_____

_____

_____

_____

_____

_____

_____

_____

_____

_____

FIRST RESORT

Hand shaking, she signs the form, tucks folder
into file drawer, closes her eyes, exhales
long and slow.
This was a tough one.
How do you persuade an alcoholic with
three children, whose incarcerated husband
might not be the father of her baby,
that choosing life is the best way forward?

Did I miss something? Maybe I should have …

She shakes her head, face sinking to cupped hands
as tears erupt. **Oh Lord!** *she cries out,*
and finds herself

at the throne of grace, before the One

who named the distant stars, who spoke Earth
into being, who breathed life into man,
the One who writes all our days into his book
before they come to be, the only One

with power over the grave, and even

as she struggles to find words, her heart
is turned to peace and the answer
is released.

Your Secret Strength

You're on the board of your local PRC, and some tough decisions lie before you. What's your first step?

You're a volunteer about to speak with a young woman who's determined to have an abortion. How do you prepare?

A fundraising event is coming up. The director shares that giving is down and the center needs a financial miracle. What can you do?

Prayer is your secret weapon. It's your invisible source of ongoing help.

Always essential for the daily Christian life, prayer is even more critical when you work or volunteer for a frontline ministry. You can't do this work without it, any more than you can get through a day without air or water.

Never underestimate the power of what God can and will do as you partner with him in prayer. Christians are often guilty of treating prayer as a last resort, but prayer needs to be the first response to difficulty.

Prayer moves mountains. Prayer sets captives free. Prayer sets God's answers in motion, which go beyond what we can think to ask or imagine.

And prayer changes us.

Human beings are fragile. We have many needs and many limitations. That doesn't concern God one bit. Our neediness makes room for his provision. Where we are empty, he wants to fill us. Where we are weak, he wants to be our strength. Where we are weary, he wants to lift us up. And where we lack, he loves to supply.

God wants to hear from you. He wants to give you joy. He loves to take care of you, your needs, and the concerns you bring to him. Lack of eloquence doesn't bother him at all.

1 Thessalonians 5:16 reminds us, "Rejoice always; pray without ceasing." So talk to God about the needs of your center. Seek him when

you don't know what to say to a client. Express your concerns to him about the young couple you're mentoring. Ask him to help you round up sponsors for the Walk for Life.

At our clinic, we place a golden stone inside a clear vase each time we see a miracle. Financial provision, a baby's life saved, a mother delivered from meth addiction, a young father getting a job, a woman healed from a past abortion—watching requests turn into praises is a powerful encouragement to continue praying.

Exercise your secret strength, and watch your faith grow. Your prayer ministry is more vital than you know.

"Rejoice always, pray without ceasing, give thanks in all circumstances; for this is the will of God in Christ Jesus for you." —*1 Thessalonians 5:16-18*

Going Deeper

Consider creating a visual reminder of how God answers prayer in your life. It could be a special journal to write in, smooth stones to write on with a marker, or slips of colored paper placed in a jar. What is your favorite idea for a reminder of God's faithfulness and a cue to continue praying?

_____

_____

_____

_____

_____

_____

_____

_____

_____

_____

IN THE DOLDRUMS

I don't mean to complain, Lord, but
it's been three weeks since I got to talk
to a pregnant girl and even then she
wasn't worried about it. I thought

you were calling me to something
exciting and meaningful. If I spend
one more Tuesday afternoon bundling
diapers and filing, I don't think
I can do this anymore.

I'm willing to serve, really I am,
but it's hard to do menial jobs
when all I want, so very much,
is to save a life.

While We Wait

Imagine you're a sailor on a ship two hundred years ago. You just survived a storm on the open seas. The howling winds, mountainous waves, and darkened skies are behind you. But now you face an entirely different danger.

You're stuck in the doldrums.

No wind at all. The ship sways listless on a flat sea, sails hanging limp, sun beating down. Day after day, you hear the creak and groan of the ship rocking side to side, going nowhere. Precious provisions are running low. Everyone is slowly going mad with the wait.

Waiting is a common trial in ministry. The missionary spends precious years in the jungle learning the customs of villagers before they're open to his message. The urban outreach team member must earn the trust of the inner-city people he is trying to reach.

Volunteering or working at your local PRC, you'll have exciting and rewarding opportunities to minister. A girl you talk to changes her mind about abortion and carries her baby. You share your faith with a young father who is ripe for the gospel. A young couple you're mentoring decides to get married instead of just living together.

Such moments are wonderful. They sustain us through the difficult times Jesus assured us would come. And sometimes hardship comes in the form of the doldrums.

Not every day brings a great victory. Days or even weeks may go by without the opportunity to talk to a single client, let alone to save a life. That can be discouraging, especially once you've experienced the thrill of a satisfying outcome.

Ministering at a PRC can be compared to working on a fire crew. Most members of the crew are volunteers. Everyone works together to be as prepared as possible for putting out fires and saving lives.

But much of the time, things are quiet. Hours are filled with maintenance work. Fire trucks need to be waxed, the crew needs to be fed, drills need to be practiced. All these activities may seem like a monotonous waste of time to the cadet who's eager to jump on that roaring fire engine, siren wailing, to get to the scene where he could save a life.

The doldrums call for endurance. In Hebrews 10:35, the writer exhorts us to persevere: "Do not throw away your confidence, which has great reward. For you have need of endurance, so that when you have done the will of God, you may receive what is promised."

God is more interested in our character than our comfort. He wants to form the image of Christ in us, and he very much wants to reward us for a job well done. Even on days when we set aside time for ministry, but all we end up doing is menial tasks, he is at work in us.

He's preparing us for the day when the fire alarm rings.

"We rejoice in our sufferings, knowing that suffering produces endurance, and endurance produces character, and character produces hope, and hope does not put us to shame, because God's love has been poured into our hearts through the Holy Spirit who has been given to us." **—Romans 5:3-5**

Going Deeper

The next time you feel bored by behind-the-scenes tasks, do two things: express gratitude to God for his promises, which are yours through endurance, and then ask him for people to come into the center during your hours of volunteering. He wants us to take ownership of our calling in this way, and he loves to answer that prayer.

_____

_____

_____

_____

_____

_____

_____

_____

_____

_____

CAUGHT IN THE ACT

They shove me down hard into a crumpled heap
at the Teacher's feet. I spit blood and gravel,
stare at the foamy red flecks. I don't dare
look up. My heart slams hammer blows,
my mouth is sandpaper. They have dragged me here
shouting with self-righteous indignation.
I am a dead woman.

I sweat. The hems of their robes encircle me.
Sandals crunch on sharp pebbles. They want
the Teacher to make a judgment. He bends down
to write, flesh of fingertip tracing delicate trails
through powder and grit. He straightens, says,

The sinless one among you, go first.
Throw the stone.

He bends to write more. I can't breathe.
Blood roars through my ears. I tense against
the certain strike of stone. Eternity passes.
Leather grinds gravel again. The circle breaks open;
they scatter, left and right. I am free, alone
but for the Teacher.

Woman, where are they? Does no one condemn you?

I shake my head, relieved, bewildered. **No one, Master.**
His eyes find mine. My heart skips a beat. What if he...
if he is sinless, he has the right to...
His gaze is clear and steady, his voice
a gentle strength.

Neither do I. Go on your way.
From now on, don't sin.

The Pain of the Past

When God calls us into the life-affirming mission, the passion he ignites in us reflects his own. As we move into this topic, we'll touch on a sensitive issue that may apply to you—and if it doesn't, it probably applies to someone you know.

According to the Guttmacher Institute, at least half of American women will experience an unintended pregnancy by age forty-five; one in ten women will have an abortion by age twenty, one in four by age thirty, and three in ten by age forty-five. In addition, nearly half of pregnancies among American women in 2011 were unintended, and about four in ten of these were terminated by abortion. Approximately 1.06 million abortions were performed.[1] The statistics for men involved in abortion decisions are also high.

If you've personally experienced abortion, you're not alone.

Healing is possible for every post-abortive woman and man. There are safe places to deal with the pain of the past. Like other issues, healing from abortion must take place on two levels.

Many people who go through abortion talk to God about their pain and regret, and they have accepted his forgiveness on a personal level, yet they still can't talk to others about their past choice. The burden of secret shame hasn't diminished with time.

In James 5:16, God says, "Confess your sins to one another and pray for one another, that you may be healed." Confessing sin to God is necessary and helpful, but this Scripture indicates that we need to confess our sin to others as well.

This is a frightening prospect. Sharing our secrets takes a great deal of courage and also requires discernment. It takes a trustworthy person to listen and help you through this process.

Many PRCs are equipped to help people overcome the pain of a past abortion. Trained counselors are available to come alongside the hurting and help them arrive at a place of forgiveness and freedom, a place where shame no longer rules their lives.

If you've experienced abortion and you want to volunteer or work in life-affirming ministry, you'll be invited to go through an abortion recovery program, which will enable you to minister out of pure compassion, free from the need to make up for a past abortion.

If you've had an abortion, you may be conflicted about whether abortion is permissible in certain circumstances. You may justify and rationalize your past decision to deal with the underlying guilt. Going through a post-abortion recovery program can bring tremendous relief, clear away confusion, and allow for an uncompromising stand for life.

In Part Two, we'll cover the sanctity of human life in a straight-forward manner. If you've had an abortion or been part of an abortion decision, may I encourage you to keep reading, even if some difficult emotions are stirred up at first? Jesus longs to heal you.

Christians doing life-affirming work must follow the example of Christ. His compassion draws people to him, although he never minimizes or excuses sin. Instead, he forgives sin and provides the power for people to live differently.

He already sees you as a shining trophy of his grace.

"There is therefore now no condemnation for those who are in Christ Jesus. For the law of the Spirit of life has set you free in Christ Jesus from the law of sin and death." —**Romans 8:1-2**

Going Deeper

Even after we've received Jesus's perfect sacrifice for our sins, we sometimes continue to wrestle with guilt. In what ways do you find yourself trying to make up for sins that you've already repented of?

_____

_____

_____

_____

_____

_____

_____

_____

_____

_____

_____

_____

The Call: Looking Back

We've completed our first ten days together. You've dipped your toes into the river, then allowed the water to play around your ankles. The river beckons; you go knee-deep and feel the pull of the water as it goes by.

We've talked about the call of God—how Jesus interrupts us and calls us to join him on a grand adventure. We've looked at some of the excuses we use for resisting his call: We're not sure what it will cost us; we may feel inadequate, inexperienced, or still wounded or guilt-ridden by our past.

Yet we're learning that God is fashioning a masterpiece in us and through us, and that he desires to resurrect our God-dreams. He asks us to put our hand to the plow and not look back, no matter how small we feel or what trials we face.

We've seen that God loves to do what is impossible by human standards and that he has been preparing us for this adventure all along. We just didn't know it. Our responsibility isn't to know and try to control, anyway.

Our responsibility is to obey.

PART TWO:
The Cause

"Give justice to the weak and the fatherless;
maintain the right of the afflicted and destitute.
Rescue the weak and the needy;
deliver them from the hand of the wicked."
—Psalm 82:3-4

GOD IN WHOM WE TRUST

God of grace and mercy,
Father to the orphan,
refuge for the wounded,
shelter to the poor.

Love for the unlovely,
mercy for our sin,
beauty for our ashes,
found in Christ the King.

Pour us out, oh Father,
break us for the broken;
vessels of compassion,
fragrance of your Son.

Help us, Lord, to love our neighbor;
teach us how to be like Jesus.

For your sake, oh God,
turn our hearts toward justice.

May your Kingdom come,
your will be done;
may your mercy shine through us,
that a broken world would see and know
You're the God in whom we trust.

(Adapted from "God in Whom We Trust," by Samuel Maynes and Susanne Maynes, recorded on "Break of Day"
*by River City Church, CCLI # 5612608). To listen, go to **rivercitychurch.us***

Act Justly, Love Mercy

Jesus loves the church, and involvement in the local church is part of healthy Christian living. Preaching and teaching God's Word is paramount. Worship is one of the highest forms of personal and corporate devotion. But justice and mercy are outward expressions of life in Christ.

If you're anything like me, you may have allowed ministries within the four walls of the church to become your comfort zone. We can be guilty of treating Christianity like a castle, hiding out in the familiarity of church life, occasionally letting down the drawbridge for a quick trip out, and then hurrying back to the safety zone.

But there's a hurting world outside that castle. Acts of justice need to be done, and mercy must be extended. Humbly walking with God, acting justly, and loving mercy aren't optional suggestions for Christians—they're required.

So how can we be sure we're practicing what God requires?

Throughout Scripture, God commands his people to reach out to the oppressed and marginalized and to stand up for the helpless. Many specific laws in the Old Testament apply to the treatment of orphans, widows, foreigners, and others who have no rights.

We have many opportunities to reach out to those who cannot speak for themselves: Children need medicine, villages need clean water, refugees need food and a roof over their heads.

All of these are important ministries. The life-affirming mission is unique in that we are the first line of defense for every endangered human being inside the womb—millions of them.

If they aren't born, we'll have no further opportunity to minister to them.

Perhaps you've been involved in church activities for years, even decades. Your ministry within the local church is valid, important, and necessary. You've helped to build up other Christians in many ways.

Yet outside your castle, justice and mercy opportunities await.

God is calling you to be a voice for the voiceless in your own city. You want to reach out to those desperate enough to snuff out an innocent life. You want to spare that life and that mother's heart.

Joining the ranks of those in life-affirming ministry is an excellent way to act justly and love mercy at the same time. You can offer mercy to distressed mothers and ensure justice for their innocent, unborn children. You can walk humbly with God as he works in you and through you to accomplish this ministry alongside your sisters and brothers.

You can be confident that you're obeying God's command.

"He has shown you, O mortal, what is good. And what does the Lord require of you? To act justly and to love mercy and to walk humbly with your God."
—**Micah 6:8 (NIV)**

Going Deeper

Write a prayer expressing your desire to be a voice for those who have no voice.

_____

_____

_____

_____

_____

_____

_____

_____

_____

_____

_____

END OF A STORY
Psalm 139:13-16

For you formed my inward parts;
You knitted me together in my mother's womb.

A speculum is inserted into the vagina.
Painkillers are injected. A tenaculum
is locked onto the cervix to pull the uterus forward.

I praise you, for I am fearfully and wonderfully made.

The cervical opening is enlarged with dilators.

Wonderful are your works;
my soul knows it very well.

A cannula, attached to a suction machine,
is inserted into the uterus.

My frame was not hidden from you,
when I was being made in secret,
intricately woven in the depths of the earth.

The contents of the uterus are sucked out.
Forceps are used to remove any remaining fetal parts.

Your eyes saw my unformed substance;

A curette is scraped along the uterine wall
to dislodge any remaining tissue.

In your book were written, every one of them,
the days that were formed for me,

> The tenaculum is released
> and the speculum removed.

when as yet there was none of them.

> The procedure is complete.

The Heart of a Father

"Then God said, 'Let us make man in our image' … so God created man in his own image; in the image of God he created him; male and female he created them" *(Genesis 1:26-27)*.

After fashioning the heavens, the earth and all other living creatures, creation comes to an apex—God forms one special creature different from all the rest, the only one created in his image.

Each time a sperm cell enters an ovum, a life begins. Whether this new person is male or female, dark-skinned or fair, blue-eyed or brown-eyed, short or tall—these attributes are already determined at conception. Psalm 139:16 poetically describes the unique destiny God has planned for each person he creates—but it also confirms a scientific fact. The DNA code for each human being is set in place from the beginning.

Every unborn person brings delight to the heart of our heavenly Father. Every abortion is an assault on one of his precious image-bearers.

Thousands of years ago, Israel's pagan neighbors worshiped a god named Molek by heating up a large iron statue of the god with fire, and then placing their newborn children on its iron arms to be burned to death. God vehemently forbids his people to practice such unthinkable evil *(Leviticus 20:2-5; 2 Kings 23:10; Jeremiah 32:35)*.

Abortion is less visible and more private than these ancient practices, but no less destructive to the innocent victim. Nor is it any less reprehensible to God.

God calls us to take a stand for justice and to defend the innocent. As John Ensor says in *Answering the Call*, "Among all human life, God especially cherishes innocent human life. … Among all forms of innocent human life, God especially treasures children. … Among all the ways that innocent children bring delight, God especially delights in fashioning children in the womb."[2]

Standing up for the innocent unborn isn't optional for God's people. Although it has become acceptable, abortion is one of the great moral evils of our time and our nation. Ensor goes on to say, "Among all the offenses of man, the greatest offense is shedding innocent blood. …

Among all the ways men shed innocent blood, the most offensive is child sacrifice."[3]

There's no easy way to state this painful truth: abortion is child sacrifice. Just as in ancient times, an innocent life is offered in exchange for the perceived benefit of another person. Circumstances are weighed against personhood, and personhood loses. In Jeremiah 7:31, God says of this travesty that he neither commanded it, nor has it even entered his mind.

Let's work together to see more life stories written out fully, as the Author of life—the Father of us all—intended.

"And you took your sons and your daughters, whom you had borne to me, and these you sacrificed to them to be devoured. Were your whorings so small a matter that you slaughtered my children and delivered them up as an offering by fire to them?" —**Ezekiel 16:20-21**

Going Deeper

Imagine how a father would react if his infant son or daughter were abducted and killed. Now consider how our Father God feels about the violent destruction of his most vulnerable, beloved children. Take some time and allow your heart to meditate on God's anguish. What do you feel?

_____

_____

_____

_____

_____

_____

_____

_____

_____

_____

CONTINUOUS LOOP

Your image moves
on the screen as you float
in a quiet ocean of grey,
waving and kicking tiny
limbs, sucking your thumb,
blissfully unaware.

Your mother has gone, her
lovely young face clouded
with a dark resignation.
She left the pictures here, left
the imprint of your soul
re-playing on the machine.

Your innocent dance repeats,
a mesmerizing pattern.
Your heart beats fast
as a kitten's. I can't turn off
the recording. You will
cease to exist.

A Life or Death Decision

When an abortion-minded woman meets her baby for the first time via ultrasound at a pregnancy center, she is twice as likely to choose life than she would be after receiving pregnancy-options counseling only. [4] This fact highlights the vital role which sonography plays in the life-affirming mission.

However, the astonishing mother-to-child connection provided by ultrasound doesn't always prevent a death decision.

Most women don't choose abortion lightly. Often their decision is due to stress, fear, or even coercion. Abortion providers appeal to women with language such as "if you decide abortion is right for you …" Some women even say they have prayed about whether they should have an abortion.

As Christians, we must understand that abortion is *never* right in the eyes of a holy God. It is always a violent, unjust, evil deed committed against an innocent, helpless human being.

A story in 2 Kings chapter 6 illustrates this principle. In this story, the city of Samaria has been under siege so long that its starving citizens resort to cannibalism. An angry woman cries out to the king for justice. One day, she and another woman agree to cook and eat her son. The next day it is the other woman's turn to give up her son—but she has hidden him, refusing to uphold her end of the bargain. The king is appalled by the woman's story and what it reveals about the wretched condition of his people.

This gruesome tale begs a question: is it permissible for a desperate, starving mother to consume her child so she herself can live a few more days? Is it any more permissible for a pregnant woman to victimize her unborn child to ease her distress?

I understand abortion is wrong, you may think, but how can we help a woman in crisis see the truth about what she's considering? Let's frame a response to this dilemma by using the example of a woman contemplating suicide.

Ending one's life also violates God's moral law. But if a woman is hopeless enough to consider suicide, telling her it's morally wrong does nothing to change her perspective or save her life. Likewise, simply preaching the truth to a woman considering abortion doesn't help either her or her child.

The mother in this Bible story needed hope. So do the women that come into PRCs every day. God wired women to need emotional support. When loving Christians come alongside a mother in crisis, she feels she has someone in her corner. She begins to see she can carry her baby to term. It will not be the end of the world for her.

And the world won't end for her baby either, because someone reached out with compassion.

"There is a way that appears to be right, but in the end it leads to death."
—Proverbs 14:12 (NIV)

Going Deeper

How have the laws allowing for abortion dulled our national conscience to this sin? Explain why making something legal doesn't make it moral.

_____

_____

_____

_____

_____

_____

_____

_____

_____

_____

_____

DESTINY DENIED

A verdict has been reached: you
are a problem which cannot be overcome.

We have a legal solution for these
dilemmas; we invade your
warm and silent sanctuary
and pull you out of this world.

You have dark brown hair with a cowlick
in the front, and blue eyes that sparkle
with mischief. You are always late for soccer
practice and leave your jacket everywhere.
You love your puppy, a once-stray yellow
Lab you insisted on keeping. You speak
with the trace of a lisp and your easy laugh
bubbles out often; your energy thunders
down the hall, echoing your insatiable zest
for life.

However,
you were not expected, and the shock
of your existence is too much to bear,
therefore you have been scheduled
for termination.

You are one of the unfortunates,
not allowed among us,
not allowed
to be.

In God We Trust?

Genesis chapters 1-3 provide insightful history about how human beings relate to God. In three short chapters, we go from nothing existing besides God, to a world being formed and populated with many creatures, to the fall of man and his expulsion from God's presence.

Whew! What happened? Everything was so idyllic in the beginning. Adam and Eve enjoyed paradise, happily taking care of God's beautiful creation, savoring sweet companionship with each other and the Creator.

How could things go so horribly wrong with just one conversation and a bite of fruit?

Even though God is holy, good, and perfect, and even though this utterly trustworthy God made all things for us to enjoy, even though we lacked absolutely nothing and things were perfect between him and us, we decided to cross the one boundary he had established for our own good.

What happened in the garden between God and our ancestors is what happens every time a human being breaks God's law. Our sin may take various forms—jealousy, stealing, lying, abortion—but the root issue is always the same.

We buy the enemy's lie that God is holding out on us, and we take matters into our own hands.

We decide God can't be trusted. We get greedy for just one more thing besides all the lovely gifts he has already given us. We commit high treason against the king of the universe. We slap him in the face and stab him in the heart.

Every time a baby is aborted, another human being has decided God cannot be trusted. A destiny is denied and a life is taken because, fundamentally, a mother doesn't believe God will take care of her and her baby. She can't see past her circumstances to a trustworthy heavenly Father.

God tells us clearly in his Word that child sacrifice has never even entered his mind *(Jeremiah 32:35)*. He also promises to provide for the widow and the orphan—and by extension, the single mother.

Trust is the biggest issue in a person coming to Christ in the first place. It is also our greatest ongoing battle. If we refuse to take matters into our own hands and instead choose to trust God, we'll be at peace. And others will see that God can be trusted.

"Trust in the Lord with all your heart, and lean not on your own understanding; in all your ways submit to him, and he will make your paths straight." **—Proverbs 3:5-6 (NIV)**

Going Deeper

Read the above Scripture passage aloud, and then write it below. Be aware of which direction you're "leaning" throughout the day.

_____

_____

_____

_____

_____

_____

_____

_____

_____

_____

_____

_____

DECISION

So it has come
to this;
standing alone
in the black-shadowed valley,
facing the giants of
confusion, guilt,
despair

They wait, looming,
silent and indifferent,
as fear strangles my mind

My eyes dart to the stony horizon,
hoping for some
light, some sign of rescue from
this awful
choice

Is there no
advocate?

Holding Out Hope

In doing compassionate life-affirming ministry, PRCs serve two populations. We help the helpless unborn by reaching out to their distressed mothers. Justice and mercy are two sides of the same coin.

You may have some concerns about taking an uncompromising life-affirming position, wondering if you'll have to argue that position or talk women out of having an abortion. You may think, *I don't have the right to tell her what to do.*

On the other hand, you may be full of zeal to save lives, eager to educate women about why abortion is wrong.

The responsibility of Christians upholding the life-affirming mission is to come alongside a woman in crisis to offer her emotional support and accurate information. The decision about an unplanned pregnancy is hers to make, not ours.

If she chooses to carry her child to term, a PRC offers her resources. If she chooses to terminate, we show mercy rather than judgment. Being fully life-affirming and compassionate toward those considering abortion isn't contradictory. In fact, we must be both. The Lord we serve is full of grace and truth *(John 1:14).*

The woman caught in the crossfire of a pregnancy decision is in a difficult, confusing position. Our culture screams at her, *You have a right to end this pregnancy!* Her conscience and her heart tell her otherwise. But she feels overwhelmed and hopeless, and abortion looks like the only solution.

Because our government has legalized something which God's law forbids, this woman is forced to play God with her child's life. How can she make such an enormous decision? Can she control or even predict how her own life will go, let alone her child's? No woman is wired to handle the devastating responsibility of deciding whether her child should or should not live.

We want to offer support to a woman in the valley of decision so she doesn't have to damage her soul and body to wiggle out of a tight spot.

Decisions made out of desperation have a way of complicating things further. The best decisions are made from a perspective of hope, not despair. Hope is what we offer: hope to get through a pregnancy, hope to raise a child, hope to pursue dreams, and the biggest hope of all—the hope of eternal life.

We are emissaries of Jesus, full of grace and truth, holding out hope. We ensure that every woman knows she has an Advocate.

"Hope deferred makes the heart sick, but a desire fulfilled is a tree of life."
—Proverbs 13:12

Going Deeper

Think about a serious moral decision you had to make. How did your level of hope correspond with the choice you made? Reflect on how this relates to a woman in an unplanned pregnancy.

_____

_____

_____

_____

_____

_____

_____

_____

_____

_____

_____

_____

_____

NOT A PRODUCT

*She falters, eyes brimming with
the memory. The rough hands,
the stench of sweat, the hissed
threats as she struggled.*

*And afterward. The positive test,
the difficult decision. The family
she selected. The bittersweet joy
as she carried and released.*

*She offers a brave smile, wipes
a tear from her cheek.* **I'm sorry,
I don't know why I'm crying.
I'm so glad my little girl
is alive.**

A Tough Topic

When we speak to women facing a pregnancy decision, we usually ask, "What do you think about abortion in general?"

Some women say they're against it. Others say it's a woman's choice. By far, the answer we hear most often is, "I'm not for it personally, but I wouldn't judge someone else who chose it—especially if it was because of rape or incest."

Perhaps this is the one circumstance that causes you to question a 100-percent life-affirming stance. If you're a mercy-motivated person, you may wonder, *Isn't it cruel to ask a woman to go through pregnancy and have the baby in this case?* Christians must give careful consideration to three aspects of this issue.

First, by allowing for abortion in the case of rape or incest, we're saying it's permissible to kill an innocent human being for the sin of his or her father. The Bible is clear on this matter. Deuteronomy 24:16 says, "Fathers shall not be put to death because of their children, nor children put to death because of their fathers. Each one shall be put to death for his own sin."

No matter the circumstances of that little girl or boy's conception, it's not his or her fault. Two wrongs never equal a right. The only path forward with God's blessing is allowing the innocent to live.

This leads to a second concern. If we allow for abortion in the case of rape, we're saying we know better than God. Romans 8:28 says, "And we know that in all things God works for the good of those who love him, who have been called according to his purpose" (NIV).

Every conception, including those due to rape or incest, takes place under the rule of a sovereign God. That doesn't mean it was God's will for the ugliness of rape to occur; it means he still makes all things beautiful in his time.

History abounds with stories of those who were born in adverse circumstances. Abraham Lincoln was born into abject poverty. Helen Keller was deaf and blind from toddlerhood. Jesus himself was born in a dirty cave under a cloud of rumors about his origin. Who are we to thwart God's good plans for a human being, regardless of how his or her life began?

Finally, does abortion help a woman who has experienced the nightmare of sexual violation? She has already been victimized and traumatized. Abortion creates another trauma. Women who have experienced both consistently testify that abortion feels worse than rape. "I didn't feel guilty for the rape," says one survivor, "but I did about the abortion."

Pregnancies as a result of rape or incest are rare. They represent well under 1 percent of unplanned pregnancies.[5] Even in those difficult few cases, aborting the child fails to help the mother.

What if abortion is necessary to save the mother's life? As it turns out, medical science does not support this idea, regardless of how noble it may sound: "… Only a small percentage of late-term abortions are done with the sole intent of saving the mother from dying from complications with pregnancy. But even that small number of 'lifesaving' abortions is questionable, because the best medical evidence reveals that of the few women who die of disease while pregnant it appears there's not even one cause of death abortion can prevent."[6]

Abortion makes empty promises, including the empty promise to save mothers' lives. No matter how tough the dilemma, ending the life of a preborn child is not the solution.

"The Lord called me from the womb, from the body of my mother he named my name." —Isaiah 49:1

Going Deeper

According to the above verse, as well as Jeremiah 1:5, when does God begin to pay attention to an individual life? Spend some time in quiet worship, thanking God for how long he has watched over you personally.

_____

_____

_____

_____

_____

_____

_____

_____

_____

_____

_____

_____

AT THE FAMILY PLANNING CLINIC

Six of us wait in recovery
on cold vinyl chairs, Kleenex
on one side, Kotex
between our legs.

The wall is covered with empty
heart shapes so we can write good-bye
to our babies.

No one speaks. Everyone weeps
except one girl staring
at her cell phone, face
hard as flint.

A woman in scrubs comes in.
I ask her about the pain.

You shouldn't have any problems.
You are free to leave.

I want to say, ***Pain is now***
my universe. I am not free.

But she won't listen. She wants
to think I have sufficiently

recovered.

Until No More Women Cry

She looks straight at me and bluntly tells me about the abortion. Ten years later, she's still angry at herself and the others involved. It's a sad story, one I've heard too many times.

Abortion offers itself as a short-term solution to a woman's dilemma. It dangles in front of her, the promise of an eraser that will make the pregnancy go away and make her life as it was before.

It's a false promise.

Women are wired to nurture. Men are wired to protect. When men and women go against their natural God-given inclination to nurture and protect their children, something fundamental shifts inside.

Our society's solution to the problem of an unplanned pregnancy takes a radical departure from the path of God's blessing. When a woman says yes to abortion, she invites death into her being. She doesn't see the high price tag attached to her decision—not only for her baby, but also for herself.

Sandy had a goal of pursuing higher education. She was in a floundering relationship when she realized she was pregnant. Because of her academic goals and the lack of support from her boyfriend, she terminated the pregnancy.

The abortion derailed her. She tried to achieve the goals a baby would have prevented, yet she couldn't concentrate enough to study. She was depressed. She felt bitter toward her ex-boyfriend, terrified her family would discover her secret, and utterly alone.

Lisa faced a similar dilemma. Her relationship with her boyfriend was on the line—he said that unless she had an abortion, they were through. Her parents had threatened to cut off her college money and throw her out of the house if she ever got pregnant. Lisa thought hard about abortion, but chose life.

Today, Lisa's parents and her ex-boyfriend are smitten with her preschool daughter and love to spend time with her. Lisa is doing well in college and exudes a confidence she lacked when I first met her.

I have yet to hear a woman say, "I have fond memories of my abortion. It really changed my life for the better." On the other hand, countless stories testify of a baby's birth bringing joy to a young mother, helping her grow up, and even healing her family. Taking the path of life brings blessing in a way that a death decision never could.

This is why we reach out to help distressed mothers and their pre-born children. As the signs held at pro-life vigils often declare, we will do this ministry "until no more babies die and no more women cry."

"The blessing of the Lord makes rich, and he adds no sorrow with it."
—Proverbs 10:22

Going Deeper

Read and memorize the verse above. How does mankind's "answer" of abortion add sorrow instead of blessing when it comes to unplanned pregnancies?

_____

_____

_____

_____

_____

_____

_____

_____

_____

_____

_____

_____

LETTING GO LULLABY

Before you saw the golden light of day,
before you knew my face, you slipped away;
before I heard the sound of your cry,
it suddenly came time to say good-bye.

I know I'll never watch you run and play,
and change with every season of the year,
and I can't bring you back to be with me;
but someday where you are is where I'll be.

Yet how my empty arms ache to hold you;
and oh, my little one, I'll miss you so.
But Jesus is the one who holds you now;
this sweet assurance helps me let you go.

Before you ever saw the golden light of day,
before you knew my face, you slipped away;
and I can't bring you back to be with me;
but someday where you are is where I'll be.

Adapted from "Letting Go Lullaby" by Susanne Maynes, recorded by River City Church, CCLI# 7079436.

Comforted to Comfort Others

Along with sharing the gospel, the main mission of life-affirming ministry is the effort to save babies' lives and help women and men facing pregnancy decisions. Surrounding that core mission are related ministries you can also be a part of.

Because of what you've been through, you may be able to comfort a young woman grieving a miscarriage or walk someone through the dark valley of postpartum depression. You may be able to help women receive forgiveness and freedom following a past abortion. You may be able to mentor a young couple who are floundering as parents.

God has a way of turning our pain into healing for others.

The work is plentiful and varied. God knows which gifts you have and how your life experience has equipped you to help others. He likes to surprise and delight us with special opportunities to partner with him in his redemptive work.

Years ago, I experienced two miscarriages. Those were difficult times, but now I have the opportunity to come alongside other women who feel similar pain. I'm blessed to walk with others through that valley, knowing the importance of comfort and understanding during that particular season of grief.

One of our volunteers came alongside a teen who was making the beautiful, but difficult, choice to place her child for adoption. The volunteer was well able to minister to this young lady and her mother during that season because her daughter had made that choice years before. God had equipped her.

I've spoken to numerous young men who have come to the PRC with their girlfriends. These young fathers have their own fears and concerns during an unplanned pregnancy. Some have even called or come in by themselves because they're desperately trying to save their baby's life, but the mother is insisting on abortion.

By giving me three grown sons, God has equipped me for these conversations. I've had the privilege of praying with some young fathers and sharing encouragement from the Scriptures with them. They've been receptive to God's love.

If you're a father, you have a wealth of wisdom you can offer a teenager whose girlfriend had a positive pregnancy test.

Or maybe you're a mother who has learned how to deal with toddler temper tantrums, or your marriage has been healed, or you've learned about substance abuse because of a family member's struggles.

Maybe you're a single person who has faced an unplanned pregnancy in the past.

Whatever you've been through, God will make good use of your life experience. Offer it to him and watch him put to use what he's already equipped you for.

"Blessed be the God and Father of our Lord Jesus Christ, the Father of mercies and God of all comfort, who comforts us in all our affliction, so that we may be able to comfort those who are in any affliction, with the comfort with which we ourselves are comforted by God."
—2 Corinthians 1:3-4

Going Deeper

Prayerfully review some of your painful experiences, whether big or small. In what area can you comfort someone else because of the way God has comforted you?

_____

_____

_____

_____

_____

_____

_____

_____

_____

_____

_____

_____

HARVEST

The pale prairie undulates for miles
under warm summer sun. Grain stands
shoulder high; ripe, heavy heads nod
with soft breezes, swelled with promise,
waiting for slice of sickle.

So many whitened fields, so vast
a harvest to gather, winnow, store.
So few workers for the task.

Therefore pray earnestly to the Lord
of the harvest to send out laborers
into his harvest.

Here I am, Lord. Send me.

Homeland Missionaries

"I've never heard of that. This is new information to me." The young woman sitting across from me looked astounded, but not disbelieving. I had just told her about the resurrection of Jesus Christ.

In our post-Christian culture, we can no longer assume the average American knows the basic facts of our faith.

Let's define evangelical Christians as those who believe that the Bible is God's true Word, that Jesus died on the cross for our sins, that individuals need to be personally converted, and that belief in the gospel needs to be expressed outwardly. The percentage of our population that fits this description is shrinking, while the number of those who embrace a post-Christian worldview is rising.

According to the Barna Group, "If an individual meets 60 percent or more of a set of factors, which includes things like disbelief in God or identifying as atheist or agnostic, and they do not participate in practices such as Bible reading, prayer, and church attendance, they are considered post-Christian. Based on this metric, almost half of all American adults (48%) are post-Christian."[7]

As you consider this reality, listen to Paul's words in Romans 10:14: "How then will they call on him in whom they have not believed? And how are they to believe in him of whom they have never heard? And how are they to hear without someone preaching?"

We need to see our country as a mission field.

When the infamous Roe v. Wade law was passed in 1973, Christians scrambled for a way to counteract the legal destruction of unborn babies. At the same time, church leaders Francis Schaeffer and Billy Graham met to discuss how this travesty could actually further the spread of the gospel. As a result of such pioneer vision, two organizations came into being which serve as umbrellas for PRCs: Care Net and Heartbeat International. (Later, another affiliate was formed to oversee medical services: the National Institute of Family and Life Advocates, or NIFLA.)

Along with saving babies' lives, the other reason PRCs exist is to offer the good news of salvation through faith in Jesus Christ. When we sit down to talk about a pregnancy decision or to mentor a young parent, we look for opportunities to explain this good news.

Your call to this ministry includes being a witness to God's truth and what he has done in your life. If this sounds a little intimidating to you, take heart. Where God guides, God provides. When Jesus gave the Great Commission to his disciples in Matthew 28:19-20, he also said, "I am with you always, to the end of the age."

Jesus is with you, helping you share the good news about him. And many centers provide specific evangelism training opportunities to strengthen your confidence and equip you with effective tools.

Picture yourself talking with a young woman or a young man who has never heard a clear presentation of the gospel. What's the worst thing that could happen to you? You might feel foolish or experience the sting of rejection. But what's the worst thing that could happen to them?

The stakes are high. The fields are ready to harvest. With God's help, you can do this.

[Jesus said,] *"Look, I tell you, lift up your eyes, and see that the fields are white for harvest."* —**John 4:35**

Going Deeper

Using the acronym BEST as a guide, write a few sentences about your life before you met Jesus events that led you to him, the moment you experienced salvation, and your life today. Aim for an elevator-speech summary, briefly explaining how your life looked before and after you met Jesus. If you grew up going to church, explain how he became real to you.

This is your testimony—the truth of what Christ has done in your life. Commit it to memory, and watch for opportunities to share it.

_____

_____

_____

_____

_____

_____

_____

_____

_____

AFTER THE VICTORY

I am Elijah under the broom tree,
stricken. I run for my life, run
forty days on the food you gave me.
It is impossible to do your will.
What can I offer such power?
You are a tempest that tears,
an earthquake that shakes, a fire
that consumes my tiny spark
as mere tinder for your blaze.

   I am not enough. You are
   too much. Terrified heart, I hide
   in a dark, empty cave

      until you come,
      your silence whisper-thin,
      to quiet me.

Mission Impossible

The fundraising banquet generated miraculous results. We raised twice as much money as we had collected the previous year, and I felt excited about saving more lives. When depression hit a few days later, it threw me for a loop.

Taking up the life-affirming banner can feel like an impossible task. Is it rewarding? Yes. Is it significant to God's heart? Absolutely. Is it easy? No promises there.

In 2 Corinthians 7:5, the apostle Paul describes the pressures he and the other apostles constantly faced, both internally and externally.

During one week at our center, we did pregnancy tests and ultrasounds for three women with addiction issues, filed two reports with the sheriff concerning minors, celebrated because one abortion-minded woman changed her mind, and mourned because another one had ended her pregnancy. It wasn't an unusual week.

Added to the situations we face within our doors is the external pressure from a society that objects to God's law concerning the unborn. Ours isn't a popular cause. We must be aware that fake clients have gone into PRCs with the express purpose of discrediting our whole movement. We are warned by our affiliates to stick to policies and procedures due to the legal trouble that could come our way.

Trouble within, and trouble without.

We are fragile human vessels. Our emotions go up and down; our capacity to care is stretched to the limit. This isn't work that can be accomplished in our own strength. It's too big. If we are to accomplish what God has called us to do, we must continually rely on him for the grace to do it.

Even keeping this in mind, at times you may feel overwhelmed. You may want to give up and run away from God's call.

He understands. "As a father shows compassion to his children, so the Lord shows compassion to those who fear him. For he knows our frame; he remembers that we are dust" *(Psalm 103:13-14)*.

When we reach the end of our rope, God doesn't roar at us or shake us. He quiets us with a whisper, reminding us of the truth and filling our vulnerable hearts with encouragement again.

Take heart. What is impossible for man is possible with God.

"And behold, the Lord passed by, and a great and strong wind tore the mountains and broke in pieces the rocks before the Lord, but the Lord was not in the wind. And after the wind an earthquake, but the Lord was not in the earthquake. And after the earthquake a fire, but the Lord was not in the fire. And after the fire the sound of a low whisper." —*1 Kings 19:11-12*

Going Deeper

Think of a time you cried out to God or hid from him because a ministry assignment became too overwhelming. How did you receive his comfort and hope?

_____

_____

_____

_____

_____

_____

_____

_____

_____

_____

The Cause: Looking Back

You've ventured a little further into the river now. The water rushes by at mid-thigh level, its pull more insistent. Fixing your eyes on the opposite bank, you search for solid footing on the slick, uneven riverbed. Twenty days. You're halfway to your goal.

For the last ten days, you've immersed yourself in what God says in his Word about the sanctity of human life. You've read and reflected on one of the most critical issues of our time, and studied the Scriptures on a topic that society considers inflammatory.

This is no tiptoe through the tulips. You're brave for coming this far.

Now that you understand clearly how much God treasures every human being he has created, your confidence has grown. You see that common rationalizations given for abortion—arguments that previously left you wavering—don't stand up in God's court of law. You're certain that abortion is always a violent crime against an innocent person; therefore, it's always a sin, and it always grieves the heart of our heavenly Father.

Knowing God's passion to protect every little one ignites your own heart. You must stand up for the helpless and be a voice for those who have none. You can never let a conversation go by on this topic without prayerfully engaging in it and speaking the truth in love.

At the same time, your sensitivity to women and men who have experienced abortion is heightened. You understand a little better why and how they were driven to make such a choice. You realize that judging others doesn't draw them toward Jesus.

You're learning that being life-affirming goes hand in hand with reaching the lost.

PART THREE:
The Culture

*"I have become all things to all people,
that by all means I might save some."*
—1 Corinthians 9:22

FOR HER SAKE

*We are keepers of secrets locked
in hard metal files, guardians
of password-protected stories. We know
about her twenty-nine sexual partners,
the years of meth addiction, her dream
of owning a hair salon, the small apartment
she shares with her boyfriend
and his cousin.*

*We are bearers of burdens too great
for one to manage alone. We heft
the weight of anguish, fear, despair,
if only for an hour, so she can breathe
and think. So she can hear Wisdom
call her name, show her the way
forward. So she can know
what she carries inside.*

*We are the voice calling in her
wilderness, speaking truth, holding out
hope; we are an oasis slaking
her thirst, offering refuge. She will leave
on the path of her choosing. We will
bless and release, pray and believe
one day she will return,
child in hand.*

Wisdom at the Crossroads

When I first started volunteering at a PRC, I pictured helping nice, middle-class girls who had gone too far with their steady boyfriends. My insulated church life hadn't prepared me to face the rubble and ruin of our sex-saturated society.

Today's young woman lives in a culture that considers sex a simple transaction. Feel lonely? Find a partner for tonight. Feel disconnected from the human race? Try having sex as a way of feeling connected for a while. Angry with your ex? Have sex with someone else as revenge.

During pregnancy-options counseling, we now routinely ask women if they're uncertain about the father's identity. This is often a dangerous dilemma for the baby, since having the "wrong" father can result in a death sentence.

On the other hand, a woman in poverty may choose having babies over getting married. She wants someone to love her unconditionally, and she may have a hard time trusting men. In her world, men often land in jail, use drugs, behave abusively, and fail to provide.

As crazy as it sounds, in today's hookup culture, marriage is considered more emotionally risky than repeatedly having sex with strangers.

The average young woman who visits a PRC started having sex in her teens and has had several partners by the time she's in her twenties. Many girls become sexually active as young as twelve or thirteen; some were sexually abused as children. It's normal for a woman to have had twenty or thirty sexual partners before she reaches her thirties. At least two women told me they've had 100 partners. Others consider themselves bisexual.

In the midst of such confusion and insanity, does one voice matter? When that young woman is bombarded by lies every day about how she should steward her sexuality, will she hear someone with a different message?

In 1951, psychologist Solomon Asch conducted a series of experiments designed to demonstrate the power of conformity in groups.[8] In Asch's classic experiments, students were told they were participating in a "vision test." Unbeknownst to the subject, the other participants in the experiment were all confederates, or assistants, of the experimenter.

When the confederates provided incorrect answers, most of the students followed their lead. Interestingly, if one of the confederates gave the correct answer while the rest of the confederates gave the incorrect answer, conformity decreased dramatically.

In other words, even amid many voices repeating a lie, if one tells the truth, that one voice is enough.

We may be that lone voice crying in the wilderness, the voice of wisdom standing at the intersections of life. When a young woman is wrestling with choices about sexual activity or deciding about a pregnancy, she stands at a critical street corner of her life. The noise of the world's traffic surrounds her. She needs to hear wisdom calling above the din and chaos.

Have you been tempted to hold back in sharing the truth because you feel it won't make any difference? Don't ever underestimate the power of the truth you've shared in the life of one young woman or couple.

It only takes one lifeguard to save a life.

"Does not wisdom call? Does not understanding raise her voice? On the heights beside the way, at the crossroads she takes her stand; beside the gates in front of the town, at the entrance of the portals she cries aloud."
—**Proverbs 8:1-3**

Going Deeper

Read all of Proverbs 8 aloud. Meditate on this passage. Picture yourself as God's representative at the crossroads of life, declaring wisdom to a confused generation. What would you say to a young woman being seduced into sexual chaos?

_____

_____

_____

_____

_____

_____

_____

_____

_____

_____

WEIGHT OF THE WORLD

She comes on her work break,
wearing a McDonalds uniform,
traces of Big Mac and
stale cigarettes trailing her.

She already has three children
by two different men. She isn't sure
who the father of this one is.
It's probably her boyfriend,
but there was one time last month when
they had a fight and she stayed
with her ex overnight.

She believes in God. Her grandma
took her to church when she was young.
She hopes there is forgiveness
if this baby has the wrong father
and she terminates.

She cups the flesh-colored model
of a fetus in her palm and murmurs,
It feels so heavy.

Face to Face with Poverty

"If they don't find a place by Thursday, they'll have no place to live. They gave their rent money to their roommate, and he spent it, so now they're being evicted. We've got to help them!"

Our volunteer was frantic. She had established a good rapport with the young couple who had come in for infant-care classes. Her heart immediately went out to the young mother, who cried throughout the class session because of postpartum depression.

We referred this couple to some other Christian ministries and community agencies for their housing needs, and we set up a time for them to return for further counseling. They seemed grateful and promised to return.

The day came. They missed their appointment. We tried calling, but the number wasn't in service. We haven't seen them since.

The volunteer worried about the couple, wondering where they and their baby were sleeping. It wasn't until we talked about what generational poverty looks like that she committed this young family to God in prayer and let them go emotionally.

Those of us who have grown up in a relatively stable, secure home environment may have trouble relating to those who have learned to survive in the chaos and constant crisis of poverty. Very likely, this wasn't the first time the couple we were helping had been through a housing crisis or similar emergency.

For many of the people we serve, normal life has never been a steady paycheck and a three-bedroom home in the suburbs. A girl who grows up in a low-income household might not learn much about mutual funds, but she knows where the best yard sales are, which stores' garbage bins contain food, and how to move in half a day. Living in a car, sleeping on a friend's couch, cooking with nothing but a microwave, making do without electricity—these are familiar circumstances.

You might feel shocked, overwhelmed, or paralyzed when you first hear about an emergency like the one the young couple faced. You'll minister more effectively if you first understand what poverty looks like.

Poverty is about more than circumstances. It's a mind-set and a lifestyle. It's a form of bondage, a deceptive stronghold that keeps people in captivity, often for generations. When a legacy of poverty has been handed down through a family line to an individual, that person has a hard time seeing that life could be any other way. He or she has no other frame of reference, no role model, and therefore no hope for change.

Yet we know that in Christ people become new creations *(2 Corinthians 5:17)*. We know he has the power to break chains and work miracles. You have the privilege of offering not only a handout, but also a hand up, out of the pit of poverty. And it all happens one baby step at a time.

As Anne Pierson, Director of Ministry Services at Loving and Caring, Inc, has said, "When we solve one need of the young woman's life, then another need or adjustment is able to come to the front, and issue by issue, a life is changed."[9]

"And he who was seated on the throne said, 'Behold, I am making all things new.'" —Revelation 21:5

Going Deeper

Express thanks to God for all you have, and ask him to give you a heart of compassion for those who have far less. Ask him to show you how you can help break cycles without taking on burdens you can't carry.

_____

_____

_____

_____

_____

_____

_____

_____

_____

_____

_____

_____

UNDER HER SKIN

*Her arms are sleeves of
painstaking artwork
in turquoise, black, red
yellow; a pair of die,*

*skulls, a heart, names
on scrolls; a random
assortment of meaning
from her story so far,*

*branded into her
supple young flesh by the
boyfriend she has
been with for five months.*

*She will bear his child
inside of a year.
She will bear his mark
for life.*

Tied for First Place, Asotin County Library Poetry Contest, Clarkston, Washington, 2011.

Love Is Blind

"He put a ring on my finger," said the girl, stretching out her hand to display it. "That's all that matters to me."

"What does the ring represent?" I asked, hoping it at least signified engagement or even a wedding date.

"Oh, it's just a ring."

Commitment and covenant are foreign terms to many people we talk to. The permanent ink of tattoos generally lasts much longer than sexual relationships outside of marriage.

Many times, the young woman who needs our services has only known the father of her baby for a couple of months—just long enough to suspect she may be pregnant. She doesn't see sex as a precious treasure to be kept and guarded for enjoyment with one person for a lifetime. She sees it as something she's willing to use to keep a guy in her life—at least for a while.

In our society, sex has been devalued from its rightful place as a passionate expression of intimate love between a husband and wife. It's treated more like loose change than a treasure. *If I refuse to have sex with him, he can get it somewhere else,* thinks a young woman. She fears being alone, so she gives sex just to be held in a man's arms for a few minutes.

A relationship that treats sex so cheaply won't last. When a man sees sex as his rightful due without commitment on his part, he no longer has a motive to pursue a woman. This girl will find herself in the same situation four months down the road, wondering why she has ended up with yet another demanding, apathetic, fickle man.

The human brain is wired to chemically bond with a sexual partner. During sexual activity, a woman's brain releases oxytocin, the same hormone released during birth and breastfeeding. This chemical is a bonding agent, which acts as a powerful glue between two human beings. Every time a woman has sex with a man, oxytocin strengthens her trust in him—whether or not he deserves it.[10] Her critical-thinking skills are impaired. She can't see the flaws in her partner that her girlfriends could easily point out.

God designed oxytocin to help marriage partners minimize each other's shortcomings and to build their trust in each other over a lifetime. When a woman has multiple sexual partners, she begins to lose her ability to bond with a man—like a piece of tape used over and over. Sadly, by the time she meets someone she wants to spend her life with, her ability to stick with him may be worn out.

How do we help a woman break this cycle and value her sexuality more highly? Good questions framed positively can help: What's the best thing your sexual relationships do for you? Are your sexual relationships giving you what you want out of life? What might your life look like if you put sex on hold until marriage?

Today's teen or twenty-something has always known a sex-saturated, yet sex-dishonoring world. Thoughtful questions and a hope-filled testimony of what a healthy marriage looks like will help restore rightful value to the gift of sexuality.

"Flee from sexual immorality. Every other sin a person commits is outside the body, but the sexually immoral person sins against his own body. Or do you not know that your body is a temple of the Holy Spirit within you, whom you have from God? You are not your own, for you were bought with a price. So glorify God in your body." —1 Corinthians 6:18-20

Going Deeper

Today, many people feel that living together is no different than marriage. Based on the passage above, how is sexual sin different from other types of sin? What are some moral and practical differences between marriage and living together?

_____

_____

_____

_____

_____

_____

_____

_____

_____

_____

_____

SARAH

There was a rape,
she states blankly, choosing
words that offer a distance
from the act, making it a
fact for the files
as though it hadn't
shattered her soul into
a thousand glittering
shards,
as though Beauty was not
assaulted and Innocence not
trampled.
Still, her darting eyes soft and skittish as
a doe
bear silent witness to
the wounding.
Gently, I voice an inadequate
I'm sorry
but I want to scream
from the rooftops
for all the universe to hear,

There was a rape,
but you are still
a princess.

*Previously published in **Talking River**, Winter/Spring 2011, 70.*

Danger or Delight?

Is fire a good thing or a bad thing? Your answer will depend on the picture that comes to mind. A cozy fireplace in mid-winter is comforting and warm. A roaring inferno consuming a family home is devastating.

God created and ordained sex, then established its parameters. He meant for sex to stay in the fireplace of a lifelong covenant called marriage. When we allow our sexuality to stray outside the healthy boundary line God has set, its power for good turns destructive.

We've been warned of the consequences of misusing sex. As a culture, we haven't listened, and we suffer for it.

Today's sexual landscape is chaotic and bewildering. In the name of freedom, we've opened the door to a kind of sexual feeding frenzy that leaves victims strewn in its wake.

College students come to PRCs for pregnancy tests shortly after they land on campus as freshmen, or six weeks after attending the latest sex educator's lecture, or after a weekend hookup with a friend-with-benefits (a relationship based on casual sex with no strings attached). A teenage girl goes to a party, gets so drunk she passes out, and later has no idea which of the boys who raped her is the father of her baby.

The rates of sexual abuse and domestic violence are statistically higher in unmarried relationships, yet Hollywood portrays adultery and fornication as the desirable norm. Pornography feeds the beast of lust and further breaks down relationships. It normalizes deviant sexual behavior and ultimately profits the abortion industry.

Of course, unplanned pregnancies often result from the mess and heartache of using sex as a meaningless commodity. Abortion presents itself as the answer to this dilemma. Many times, the issue is that the baby's father is the "wrong guy," because the mother was involved with two or more men around the same time and fears being found out.

Sexually transmitted diseases and infections are rampant. With every sexual partner a woman has, she is exposed to every person he has had sex with, which means her risk of contracting an STD or STI increases exponentially with every additional partner. By the time a girl has had ten sexual partners, if each of them had the same number of partners, she has potentially been exposed to over a thousand people. She may even lose her ability to bear children and be unaware of it until she tries.

Going by reported incidents—and many go unreported—it is estimated that one out of four girls—and one out of six boys—is sexually abused by age eighteen, making a total of 42 million victims.[11] If you've been sexually injured, you're not alone.

Years ago, an ad for Virginia Slims cigarettes said, "You've come a long way, Baby," highlighting the progress women had made in smoking publicly as freely as men do. The American Lung Association later used the ad in a clever way; instead of depicting women happily smoking, they showed images of those ravaged by lung cancer.

Regarding sex, "You've come a long way, Baby"—not toward happiness, security, and love, but toward heartache, disease, and brokenness. The good news is, Jesus offers healing and the hope of a fresh beginning to every child of God who has been burned by the fire of unrestrained sexuality.

And we have the privilege of restoring hope and dignity to the princess God created.

"Can a man scoop fire into his lap without his clothes being burned?"
—Proverbs 6:27 (NIV)

Going Deeper

Many of us carry wounds from our past due to situations outside God's "fireplace" for sexuality, whether by choice or against our will. In either case, Jesus loves to heal the brokenhearted. Write out a prayer asking him to heal any wounds you may have experienced in this area.

_____

_____

_____

_____

_____

_____

_____

_____

_____

_____

_____

SIXTEEN

There is no hell, *she says.* **Hell
is right here and now.**

*Hands fidget and twist. Glazed eyes
lock with mine, daring me to care.*

*Her father won't let her leave
the house. Lots of people come
and go. She smells funny smoke,
weed, but something else too. She thinks*

*he does drugs. He sleeps a lot, yells,
throws things. Small things, mostly,
but once he threw a pan and
barely missed.*

*Cigarettes are stress relief. Also smoking
weed and having sex. She tells me*

she has a lot of hate for her father. I **believe
in God,** *she says,* **but I won't read
the Bible.**

*It says God judges bisexuals. I think
he likes me just the way I am with*

my stupid tattoos.

Your Truth, My Truth

"You can wear that cute maternity top even if you're not pregnant. I'm not gonna judge you," said the sales clerk to the customer in front of me.

Judge? I thought. *Isn't that a strong word for a simple fashion choice?*

We live in a society easily offended by any kind of judgment, good or bad. I've heard numerous young women say, "I think abortion is killing a baby." In the same breath they'll say, "I would never have an abortion, but I wouldn't judge someone else who did."

The woman who is younger than forty has never known a world where abortion is illegal, so she sees it as a morally valid choice. She swims in a cultural soup of postmodernism which has saturated her thinking. She believes it's wrong to make judgments of any kind, whether or not she goes to church or reads her Bible and prays.

In her mind, even God doesn't have the right to judge anyone.

Postmodern thinking doesn't make sense to those of us who grew up in the age of modernism. A church-going youth in the sixties and seventies faced the claims of secular humanism and evolution theory, with science being pitted against the Bible in public debates.

But the rules of the game have changed.

The postmodern thinker believes in relativism, which claims there are no absolutes. You decide whether there is a God, and if so, what he or she is like. What you sincerely think and feel matters more than either scientific research or the Bible. In other words, your truth works fine for you, but I may have a different truth. And if you judge me, you're the one in the wrong.

"The women in my church think it's wrong to live together if you aren't married," one girl told me as she rolled her eyes. "They're kind of old school." Her point of view gives little credence to the authority of Scripture or the Lordship of Jesus. She sees truth as relative.

In the absence of moral absolutes, our culture no longer defines sexual responsibility in terms of restraint. Now it's all about using birth control properly. The average young woman would "never judge" a couple that decided to move in together before marriage. Yet she feels shame over getting pregnant because she failed to get to the health department on time for this month's batch of pills. Judgment and shame still exist—the only thing that's changed is our belief about what is shameful.

How do we address such moral confusion? How do we reach a young woman who has no moral compass and whose conscience is unreliable?

Jesus says we are to be salt and light, a city set on a hill that cannot be hidden *(Matthew 5:13-16)*. We have the privilege of inviting the lost into the presence of Jesus. He is full of both grace and truth. And we have the privilege of representing him.

Instead of arguing, we can look for points of agreement and start there. We can avoid "Christianese" jargon like *saved, born again,* or *quiet time* and use language non-Christians understand. We can ask open-ended questions such as "What is it about Buddhism that attracts you?" We can show a genuine interest in the person and her story. From there, we may be able to present the gospel.

Let's stand firm on the truth as we reach out in love.

"Do not judge by appearances, but judge with right judgment."
—John 7:24

Going Deeper

According to the above verse as well as 1 Corinthians 6:1-3, describe a Christian's responsibility to judge. How do these passages encourage you to confidently agree with God when it comes to moral judgments?

_____

_____

_____

_____

_____

_____

_____

_____

_____

_____

_____

_____

TEXT MESSAGE

I'm pretty sure I'm pregnant.
OMG! R u being a drama queen?
Really? U r supposed to be my BFF.
U can't be pregnant. No way.
Right? Seriously, though, I think I am.
Did u forget your pills or something?
FYI I'm not a moron. I took the stupid pills.
Did u tell Michael yet?
No. Don't want to freak him out.
He has like three kids already, right?
Yeah. He said he doesn't want any more.
OMG. What r u going to do?
Have to find out 4 sure if I'm pregnant first.
Totally coming with u for the test.
K. Can u pick me up at 3?
Done.
KThnxBye

Understanding a Generation

You're seated in a small, private room with a nineteen-year-old named Brittney, ready to discuss her pregnancy options. You ask her to turn off her cell phone. She sits facing you, nervously twisting a strand of hair.

Brittney was born between 1982 and 2002. This makes her a member of the Millennial generation.

She's at ease in the world of constant technological advancement. She sleeps with her cell phone beside her. She never turns it off unless she's required to do so, because that makes her anxious. She doesn't want to miss anything.

Brittney spends eight hours a day on her phone and computer. Her constant electronic connection to everyone causes her fatigue and depression, but this is the world she has always known. She feels lonely inside but doesn't know why.

Brittney unconsciously treats her relationships as if they were online—where it's quick and easy to cut and paste or delete. She's good at multitasking but has trouble focusing on anything that doesn't happen instantly.

When she has a question, Brittney turns to the Internet for answers. She has several hundred Facebook friends, and she uses Google and Wikipedia to do research. Because so much information is at her fingertips, she doesn't see the older generation as necessarily wiser or more expert than she is at navigating life. Her favorite question is "why?"

She was raised by helicopter parents, so she's somewhat overprotected and pampered. For this reason, Brittney feels she should receive accolades just for trying. She likes to think of herself as a caring person, and she's interested in good causes. She avoids controversy because she doesn't want to be seen as judgmental.

How do you effectively reach out to Brittney? She needs to understand that the world is unfair and human nature is sinful. She needs to know the difference between good and bad behavior. She needs to be emotionally connected to people face-to-face, not just through social networking.

Brittney is unlikely to respond well to authoritative instruction or preaching. She won't be inclined to listen to you because you're older and have life experience.

Approach her with an attitude of gracious humility. Think of yourself as someone who's learning alongside her rather than someone who's teaching her. If you ask her the right questions and let her take ownership of the answers, she'll begin to trust you. Trust will open the door so you can be a godly influence in a life that's been shaped by the world's thinking.

"Put on then, as God's chosen ones, holy and beloved, compassionate hearts, kindness, humility, meekness, and patience." —Colossians 3:12

Going Deeper

How can you take steps to bridge the gap between yourself and a member of the Millennial generation, considering that he or she may see the church as irrelevant? What aspects of typical Millennial thinking and behavior do you especially need patience for?

_____

_____

_____

_____

_____

_____

_____

_____

_____

_____

_____

_____

_____

TURNING POINT

Metal studs pierce the flesh of her ears,
nose, lips; weapons guarding downcast eyes
that won't meet mine.

She talks about the hitting, how at first,
she looked sad. Then people asked
what was wrong, so she learned
to not look sad.

They put her in a room for three days
without food. Some days she counts
the walls around her, still.

Her dad used to take her dirt biking,
but now he has a new girlfriend. Her mom
is busy doing meth. Her boyfriend
is in jail.

She wonders what God is like. Did she
do something terrible in another life?
Is it karma?

Her boyfriend has started reading the Bible
in prison. She went online to find verses
on forgiveness.

She fingers the silver, heart-shaped key
on the necklace she found
yesterday.

What's Her Worldview?

Six of us sat in the upper-division history class. As the only girl, and a sophomore at that, I timidly suggested a spelling correction for the long German word our professor had painstakingly written on the chalkboard.

The word was *Weltanschauung,* meaning worldview. I didn't know that it had two *u*'s because I was brilliant—as my classmates feared. I knew how to spell it because my first language is German.

The young women and men who enter a PRC also have a first language when it comes to spiritual things. America is a post-Christian nation. Christians can no longer assume the average citizen shares our vocabulary or point of view. We are missionaries in our homeland. The first task of a missionary is to study the language and customs of the people he or she wants to reach.

Under "religious background" on PRC intake forms, there are check boxes for Christian, Buddhist, Wiccan, Mormon, and "other." When we meet with a young woman, we explore how she feels about God. If she shuts down in body language, voice, or expression, we change the subject. If she shows interest, we ask open-ended questions that clarify what she believes about spiritual things.

One question we avoid asking is, "Are you a Christian?" She would likely say yes, based simply on a vague belief in God or church attendance as a child.

Some people come to salvation in Christ by means of a Damascus-Road experience. The blinding light of revelation knocks them flat and everything changes. Others have an Emmaus-Road conversion, where it gradually dawns on them who Jesus really is.

When he walked the earth, Jesus said to certain people, "You're not far from the Kingdom of God." Among those we meet, some are about to receive a blinding revelation of who God is. Others are experiencing a growing awareness, which will culminate in salvation.

We attempt to come alongside and find out where a young woman finds herself on her journey of faith. Does she ever talk to God? Has she had a significant personal encounter with him? Does she have a story about being wounded by church members?

Was she raised in a home that practiced atheism, Native American rituals, or Mormonism? Does she believe in a higher power because her mother attends AA? Has she stitched together a patchwork quilt of beliefs based on hearsay and whatever feels right? Does she describe herself as "spiritual, but not religious"?

God can do astounding things in one conversation when we ground ourselves in his Word, demonstrate a genuine interest in people, and let the Holy Spirit lead.

"They said to each other, 'Did not our hearts burn within us while he talked to us on the road, while he opened to us the Scriptures?'" —**Luke 24:32**

Going Deeper

Read up on a world religion.[12] What are its basic tenets? How is it similar to Christianity? How is it different?

Observe what other religions teach about Jesus. They may consider him to be a great rabbi, an enlightened one, or a prophet, but only Christians believe he is God. The deity of Jesus is the dividing line between other world religions and Christianity.

_____

_____

_____

_____

_____

_____

_____

_____

_____

_____

_____

IMPOTENT

Last week he found her note
by the pile of crusty dishes:
I am going to do it.

Her things are gone, the stash
of bills in the small drawer
missing. She does not answer
his calls.

He lays awake at night
and stumbles through the day,
cursing, weeping, shaking fists
at silent heavens,

while she weighs the fate
of his fatherhood.

Not Always the Bad Guy

Every pregnancy, planned or not, involves a father. And men can be devastated by unplanned pregnancies and subsequent abortion decisions.

Jake came in with his teenage girlfriend, Emma, to discuss their options. Emma's mother wasn't a fan of their relationship, but Jake loved Emma and desperately wanted to marry her. Emma initially decided to carry her child. Soon after, Emma told us she'd broken up with Jake and had a miscarriage. Later, she confessed she'd had an abortion. Jake was devastated.

Tyler came to talk to us because he couldn't convince his girlfriend to come. He wanted her to carry their child to term, but she was too deeply depressed to consider anything other than abortion. Tyler said this was the fourth time one of his girlfriends had chosen abortion. More than anything else, he wanted to be a dad.

Michael and Allison were excited about her pregnancy. Within a month, she was heading for an abortion clinic against his wishes. She said she was so frightened by Michael's abusive behavior she couldn't fathom bringing a child into the situation. In desperation, Michael called us. He allowed us to pray for him and was receptive to learning more about God through this hardship.

Men aren't necessarily the bad guys when it comes to un-planned pregnancies.

It's true abortion allows men to be sexually irresponsible. It's true some young men pressure their girlfriends into an abortion, using the threat of ending the relationship as leverage. Some guys offer to pay for all or part of an abortion but refuse to offer support in terms of raising a child.

Other young fathers simply leave the burden of responsibility on the mother, saying, "I'll support whatever decision you make." This is a cop-out, yes, but haven't we been telling men that being supportive and sensitive is more important than taking responsibility?

The young father we see may come from a family trapped in gener-ational poverty, relational chaos, or alcohol and drug abuse. Perhaps his parents never married. He may have learned to solve problems with his fists rather than with good communication. Repeated patterns of family crises, run-ins with the law, and jail terms might be normal life for him because that's all he has ever known.

No matter his background or his reasons, when a man does participate in an abortion decision, he's at risk for psychological consequences similar to those for women. Years after the abortion, he may find himself feeling disconnected from his wife and children, uncomfortable in the presence of men he sees as "good," and struggling to submit to his employer.

Still, every father is created in the image of another Father. When a man cries out for the life of his child or cries out for forgiveness after an abortion, God's heart is moved. We are wise to let our hearts be moved as well and to reach out with the hope of the gospel to the hurting young men we talk to.

"Judge not, that you be not judged. For with the judgment you pronounce you will be judged, and with the measure you use it will be measured to you."
—Matthew 7:1-2

Going Deeper

Allow the Lord to examine your heart. Is there any area where you tend to judge the men who consider abortion, influence a woman toward it, or don't try to stop it?

BEFORE REDEMPTION

She launches a preemptive strike,
her words hurling accusations
at any who dare touch
the wound

My body, my choice
I did what I had to do
You are tyrants and
hypocrites

She is Mary Magdalene,
yanked on puppet strings
by demons within,
still tormented,

yet to kiss the feet
of Mercy and cry,

Rabboni

Denial and Defensiveness

I was invited to speak about the services of our clinic at a local social service agency lunch meeting. During the Q & A session, one woman challenged me, "I heard you're all about putting an end to abortion."

I felt my cheeks heat up, but simply replied, "We would always rather see a woman choose another alternative, because abortion hurts women." Instantly, the woman's eyes dropped to the floor. She probably had been through abortion. She needed grace, not an argument.

Another time, I sat in an airport reading a memoir while waiting for my next flight. The writer's wit, style, and vulnerability were exceptional. As her story unfolded, I had a growing, uneasy hunch she had experienced abortion. Sure enough, about halfway through the book, this author's pain seeped onto the pages. At one point, she described George Bush and life-affirming members of Congress in such a hostile, disrespectful way I had to lay the book aside for a half hour to calm down.

This woman's pain, though well rationalized, was clearly unresolved. She dealt with it by shifting the blame. A multitude of others among us, many of them in our churches, remain defensive about a past abortion, insisting that women should have the right to make that decision.

Freedom of choice for women has wreaked havoc in so many lives that our whole society has been deeply affected by this travesty. Post-abortion syndrome can cause eating disorders, substance abuse, depression, and suicide. The ripple effect of countless private decisions has sent shock waves throughout the whole population.

Public figures sometimes serve as unfortunate examples of the effects of abortion. Dr. Theresa Burke, author of *Forbidden Grief* and founder of Rachel's Vineyard, the nation's largest post-abortion recovery ministry, tells the stories of great personal cost paid by certain celebrities.

Judy Garland was forced to undergo an abortion by her mother and husband, who felt a baby would endanger her blossoming film career. After the abortion, Judy developed an eating disorder, became depressed, and ultimately committed suicide. The connection is worth noting.

Princess Diana had an abortion after her well-publicized affair. She too developed an eating disorder and became obsessed with helping children avoid land mines in war-torn third world countries. Intense involvement in a cause that helps children or animals is often a symptom of post-abortion syndrome.[13]

Though an abortion may be kept secret, it doesn't take place in a vacuum. When we consider that every woman has a circle of relationships, it's easy to see how one abortion could easily affect fifteen or more people. How many women still suffer over a past abortion—and how many of their loved ones, coworkers, and friends are affected along with them? How much collective damage has been done by this particular choice?

The problem is all the more complex because our society has minimized the sin of abortion—and, in doing so, has minimized its grief as well. How many women and men have been left to suffer alone? Even secular, pro-choice psychologists now say that post-abortive counseling is a necessary therapy.[14]

We stand in the chaos, speaking the truth in love to millions of Mary Magdalenes. Some are closer to breaking the chains of denial than others.

Let's stand firm for life, respond with kindness, and trust God to deliver one Mary at a time.

"Know this, my beloved brothers: let every person be quick to hear, slow to speak, slow to anger; for the anger of man does not produce the righteousness of God." —James 1:19-20

Going Deeper

Have you ever found yourself involved in a heated, defensive discussion about abortion? Describe what a more disarming approach to this difficult topic might look like:

_____

_____

_____

_____

_____

_____

_____

_____

_____

_____

_____

_____

WEARY IN WELL DOING

He hefts rough-hewn sack to bony
shoulder, bowing under weight

of seed to sow, shuffles along
furrows, scattering left to right

in sweeping semicircles, squinting
down the long field with a sigh.

Maybe this year. *He has let soil rest,*
plowed up hardened clods, stirred in

rich manure; maybe this crop
yields sweet payback for hard labor.

He crooks an elbow, wipes sweat
from his brow, glances upward

at a cloudless, silent sky.
God, I'm so very tired.

It's Not for Nothing

"But I have said, 'I have labored in vain; I have spent my strength for nothing and vanity.'" —Isaiah 49:4

At times even Jesus wondered whether his message and ministry was having any effect. That's what this prophetic passage about the Messiah reveals. Since a servant isn't above his master, it's no wonder we get weary at times.

Combating today's paradigm about the value of human life and the proper place of our sexuality is a huge undertaking. Because so many people have accepted the lies that sexual freedom means lack of boundaries and that human life is expendable if the person hasn't yet been born, Christians who tackle these issues encounter many obstacles.

We swim upstream against a powerful current of godlessness. For PRC volunteers and staff, there are days and seasons that can be discouraging. Some young women we talk to and pray for still have an abortion. Commitments to sexual purity are few and far between. The progress of a young father trying to get his children back is three steps forward, two steps back.

The work is hard. We get tired.

How do we keep going when we can't see our efforts making a difference?

When we're weary, it helps to remember the challenges we face aren't new. Christians throughout the ages have spent their lifetimes addressing the human condition with the gospel of Jesus Christ. The world's mindset is the same today as it was in the time of Noah, or Daniel, or Paul. Remember, Jesus says, "Take heart; I have overcome the world" (*John 16:33*).

The best way to take heart is to work for God, not for outcomes. There's something about putting one foot in front of the other and leaving the results in God's hands that he appreciates. He likes faith.

Faith continues to say yes and to walk out the commitment when results say nothing's happening. Faith counts God as trustworthy—willing and able to bring about the outcomes he wants long before we see them.

As you labor for the Lord, stay the course. You'll reap the promised harvest.

"And let us not grow weary of doing good, for in due season we will reap, if we do not give up." **—Galatians 6:9**

Going Deeper

If you feel weary in ministry, how have you slipped into the habit of relying on your own strength to carry out God's will? Ask him to help you get back on track, and tap into his power to carry out divine assignments.

_____

_____

_____

_____

_____

_____

_____

_____

_____

_____

_____

_____

_____

The Culture: Looking Back

The water is tugging hard now. It's more difficult to keep your balance as the cool current relentlessly rushes by, swirling up to your hips. Thirty days into this journey, you've almost reached the other shore.

You can do this.

In the last ten days, you've taken a closer look at our nation's culture. Not a pretty sight. You may have been shocked about the way sexuality is handled today. You've looked at the tragic cheapening of God's good gift of sex and the devastating effects of letting physical passions run rampant.

You've studied relativism and postmodernism, philosophies that have shaped the mind-set of Millennials. You understand that the typical young person today isn't well informed about Christianity, but to reach them, you must first earn their trust.

You've also seen pictures of lives marred by poverty and drug abuse, and you realize how this kind of background affects the spiritual condition of an individual or a family.

You now realize that our entire society has been marred by the travesty of abortion. You're developing a greater compassion for those who've been caught in its trap, even though they're still defensive. You're letting go of unloving judgments against those who've chosen abortion.

You see the amount of work that must be done for the sake of the gospel. You understand that it won't be accomplished by means of human strength but only by relying on God's grace and the guidance of the Holy Spirit.

We must lean into God and trust him to do what only he can do, one life at a time.

PART FOUR:
The Crown

*"Blessed is the man who remains steadfast under trial,
for when he has stood the test he will receive the crown of life,
which God has promised to those who love him."*
—James 1:12

FOUR YEARS LATER

You jump off the second step
from the bottom, thump, then
whirl around, grinning **Hi!**
and gallop toward the toys
in the waiting room.

Your father's girlfriend mentions
your name. She does not hear
my breath catch.

Your mother came here, back when
she dropped out of high school
to go to rehab. You were the size
of a coffee bean. She was not
going to keep you, but then

she saw you dancing
on the ultrasound screen.
She said, **Now I know**
it's a real baby.

A Holy Day

Rewarding moments come in many forms for those who minister at pregnancy resource centers.

An atheist engages in conversation about spiritual things and takes home a Bible to read for himself. A young woman who hears the gospel tells her counselor she knows she was meant to be there that day.

A young father comes in for Life Skills classes with his girlfriend. In learning about principles of marriage and relationships, he decides to work things out with his wife instead. He continues relationship classes with his wife as they work on rebuilding their marriage. Another couple who intended to move in together decides to marry instead.

These and many other encounters are significant and wonderful. Yet none of them tops the reward of seeing and touching a living, breathing baby who is in this world due to an ultrasound you performed as a nurse or a conversation you had as a pregnancy options coach.

I'll never forget my first time.

It was a Tuesday morning, my day to volunteer. Our front door swung open, and in walked a teenager I had talked to months before. During that visit, she told me abortion was probably the right choice for her.

Now she was lugging an infant seat.

Holding my breath, I pulled back the soft pink blanket to reveal an exquisite five-day-old girl. I reached out to touch her downy blonde head as she lay sleeping, feeling as though I was the one dreaming. The blanket gently rose and fell with the rhythm of her breathing. I pulled it back further to reveal perfect little arms and legs, fingers and toes.

She could have died, I thought, *yet here she is. And I got to be a part of that.* The sleeping babe stirred a bit. Her tiny mouth opened to form an *O,* then closed again. *Oh.* The right word for a holy moment.

Every baby we see at the clinic is precious, but the fragile beauty of that little girl is forever etched in my memory. That day is a sacred day on the calendar of my life.

I long for many other Christians to experience such a moment. I pray you are one who answers God's call and has the privilege of participating in this movement, which is so close to his heart.

I wish for you to have a holy day on your calendar like I do—the day you first see the fruit of your labors. I pray that the impact of those moments won't diminish with time for you or me.

May we never lose sight of the preciousness of life, and may we remember to celebrate every holy day God puts on our calendar.

"My mouth will speak the praise of the Lord, and let all flesh bless his holy name forever and ever." —Psalm 145:21

Going Deeper

When God allows you to see the results of your ministry efforts, what are some creative ways you can celebrate? Consider ideas such as a special dinner with family or friends, planting a rosebush, or hanging a plaque with a special verse that reminds you of what God did through you.

_____

_____

_____

_____

_____

_____

_____

_____

_____

_____

_____

_____

_____

GIVE AND TAKE

What sweet solace I find
here,
in the perfect space between
your little shoulder and your
plump, silken cheek;
my eyes shut tight against
life's demands, all my failures,
the ought-tos.

I bury my face
in the warm folds of your neck
and breathe deeply
of sweetness, purity,
unspoiled beginnings.

Like warm oil on a wound,
your sigh of sheer
contentment
washes over my bruised and weary
self.

Who could say
which is giver and which is taker
between us?

Previously published in **Welcome Home,** *May 1992, 8.*

The Power of a Baby

Taylor was pregnant at seventeen and still in high school. Her best friend told her, "You better not get an abortion!" Her boyfriend said, "If you keep it, we're done."

Her parents threatened her too: if she ever got pregnant, they'd kick her out and cut off her college money. So many voices shouted at Taylor that she didn't know what to do. She was strongly inclined to pursue abortion.

Brandy was only a junior in high school when she got involved with a boy her parents didn't approve of. Her pregnancy threatened to interrupt her schooling and end her cheerleading. Brandy felt she should probably have an abortion.

Amanda and Ryan were afraid. If her parents found out she was pregnant, they'd "kill her." A high-school senior, Amanda planned to attend college. She and Ryan felt it wasn't the right time for a pregnancy. They planned to keep it secret and have an abortion.

Courtney's boyfriend broke up with her. She wanted to go back to college and was fearful of disappointing her parents. She also had to continue working. Courtney felt she needed to "take care of the problem."

In all these scenarios, fear played a major role—fear of the future, of financial hardship, of interrupted hopes and broken dreams, of angry parents and ruined relationships. Yet in all four cases, the young mothers chose to carry their babies, and none of their fears materialized.

Taylor's ex-boyfriend dotes on his little girl. Her mom is a devoted grandma. And Taylor is working on her bachelor's degree, a confident young woman who has learned how to speak for herself.

Brandy decided to place her son for adoption. She continued high school, and her little boy's adoptive parents attended her cheerleading events. Amanda and Ryan married, and both have good jobs. Amanda's parents support the marriage wholeheartedly and thoroughly enjoy their granddaughter.

Courtney says her daughter is the best thing that ever happened to her, and she can't imagine a life without her. Her parents help her a great deal, and she's able to work as well as attend college again.

God always refers to a child as a blessing—no exceptions.

A baby has power. A baby can unite a family, heal wounds, and give purpose. A baby can help a floundering young woman grow up.

What a joy to watch a young mother nurture the child she thought she'd be better off without. What a privilege to watch a young woman hold and love her baby, knowing she almost made a tragic decision. What an honor to watch her receive life from the one she chose life for.

*"Behold, children are a heritage from the Lord, the fruit of the womb a reward." —**Psalm 127:3***

Going Deeper

Meditate on the verse above. In what ways is every child a blessing, even those conceived and born in difficult circumstances?

_____

_____

_____

_____

_____

_____

_____

_____

_____

_____

_____

_____

_____

MIDWIFE

I am Shiphrah, I am Puah,
I fear no pharaoh,
only Father,
Who gives me
strength and wisdom
to help you squeeze through
suffocating darkness into
blinding light

Who am I to
hold you,
slippery with water and
blood,
eyes filled with wonder,
spirit sucking in your
first breath of
Life?
Spent and undone, I
weep and laugh and marvel
at your new
beginning

You are twice born,
and I have never been more
alive

A Different Kind of Birth

"See, this answers my question," said Mandy. "I always wondered how I could trust a book that was just written by men, and this explains it. It's right here!"

The soft-spoken young woman was reading the first chapter of the Gospel of John in the new Bible I had just given her. She had come in for a pregnancy test, concerned about having a miscarriage. Mandy wanted a child, and her first and only other pregnancy had ended that way.

As she shared her fears, she said, "I don't know how you are about God and all that, but I talk to him a lot, and I've been asking him to keep this baby safe. But I don't know. Everything happens for a reason…"

The door was open for me to explore with Mandy how she related to God and whether anyone had ever explained to her the way of salvation by faith in Jesus Christ.

I explained Christianity is no guarantee of a pain-free life, that, in fact, Jesus promises we'll suffer. The difference for the Christian is God makes a specific promise to us that he'll work all things together for the good in our lives *(Romans 8:28)*.

"God never wastes our pain," I said.

Tears rolled down Mandy's cheeks. Her father had abandoned the family when she was a baby, her mother had been through several relationships, all the girls in her family had gotten pregnant at a younger age than she did, and she had already had several sexual partners.

Pain? Yes, she had a plateful. Mandy was so ready to receive the gospel that she did so before we ever got around to her pregnancy test.

God knew her biggest need. He brought her through our doors at the most opportune time. She had a partial understanding of spiritual things from a stitched-together background of various churches, but on that day she took a leap of faith and received Jesus's gift of salvation.

Mandy came in for a pregnancy test. She left a new creation in Christ. In the process of confirming the new life growing inside her, a new life began for her—a life that will last for eternity.

It's difficult to describe what it feels like to witness such a profound miracle, to be the person who catches that spiritual newborn. Perhaps the best description is found in 1 Peter 1:8, "joy that is inexpressible and filled with glory."

We taste this indescribable, glory-filled joy when we courageously hold out the truth to others. We partake in this feast because we've prepared ourselves, looked for opportunities, and taken the risk when the moment comes. Sharing the gospel with someone who's ready to hear it is like walking into an orchard, reaching up to touch a ripe peach, and feeling the heavy sweetness fall softly into your palm.

"Taste and see that the Lord is good" *(Psalm 34:8)*. He works all things for good, in your life and in the lives of those you introduce to him.

"I planted, Apollos watered, but God gave the growth."
—1 Corinthians 3:6

Going Deeper

We play various roles in sharing the gospel and seeing others come to saving faith. How has God most often used you—as a seed planter, as one who waters, or as one who reaps the grain when it's ready? Ask him for more opportunities, and be willing for him to use you in new ways.

_____

_____

_____

_____

_____

_____

_____

_____

_____

_____

_____

_____

_____

CHANGES

They sit close together, tense,
quiet. She is barely eighteen,
still a senior in high school.
He wrings his hands, eyes flickering
toward mine. **Her parents will kill her.**
We can't have this baby.

They go into ultrasound, see
their child kick and wave and
suck her thumb. They decide
to keep her.

They take months of classes, learn
of babies' growth, how to manage
money, why marriage matters.
Paradigms shift.

Two years later, we see them
with their bright-eyed toddler girl,
a thousand dollars in the bank,
gleaming golden bands on their
left ring fingers.

Breaking Cycles, Changing Lives

God has a thing about family trees. His Word contains numerous, carefully preserved genealogies. His specific promises extend throughout history by means of family lineage. God is always working to bring blessing to each family on the earth and to restore blessing when it has been lost.

But blessing can be stolen. An enemy is always lurking, eager to snatch it away.

Sadly, many of the surnames of young women and men we see are quite familiar to the policemen and nurses in our community. Poverty is a generational curse; so are addiction, crime, and despair. A young person whose family blessing has been robbed often has no instruction, no role model, no support in living a healthy, godly life.

Volunteering or working at a PRC is an effective way to break generational cycles. You can be the one God uses to free a young man or woman trapped in his or her family's negative patterns.

God's Word doesn't return to him empty *(Isaiah 55:11)*. When you facilitate a faith-based parenting class with a young mother, or lead a class on principles of marriage with a couple, or mentor a young father, you're imparting eternal truths.

We've seen significant changes in students who take the Life Skills classes at our clinic. The local courts now refer parents to us for classes when their children are removed from the home by Child Protective Services. Parents gain insight and confidence, which makes it possible for their families to be reunited.

Marriages are restored. Cohabiting couples get married. And some have come to faith in Christ.

All these wonderful changes will impact the next generation. Curses will be broken and blessing restored. If you're preparing to teach one of our classes, ask God for eyes to see what he's doing in the lives you touch.

Change doesn't come easily. Impatience can squelch our joy. We get tired of preparing for a class if the students don't show up. We may discount a step in someone's progress because we don't think it's significant.

Remember, God measures things differently than we do.

The mother of one of our students told us our series of classes was the first thing her daughter had ever completed. We might be tempted to think, *It's about time. She has a long way to go.* Or we can rejoice, thinking, *Wow, she took initiative. This is huge. She'll be encouraged to complete other things too. God is at work!*

Every time a person makes a positive change, that change is a miracle. Your kindness, perseverance, and faith can help break cycles, change lives, and transform family trees. Your contribution will impact the next generation—one life, one step at a time.

"And the things you have heard me [Paul] say in the presence of many witnesses entrust to reliable people who will also be qualified to teach others."
—2 Timothy 2:2 (NIV)

Going Deeper

Lord, I long to be an agent of the kind of transformation only you can bring. This is my prayer for someone I've taken under my wing:

_____

_____

_____

_____

_____

_____

_____

_____

_____

_____

_____

_____

_____

_____

OUT OF THE STRONGHOLD

She crouches in a cold dungeon, huddled
against old memories and long-held
beliefs. Cruel voices repeat lies, the echo

tormenting for years. **Unworthy.**
She wrestles shame, straining for
whispered truth over clamored

accusation. Hope stirs in her spirit.
A distant light catches her eye—soft,
growing brightness piercing blackest night.

And then comes the song, its sweet melody
floating to her like perfume, dispelling
dank, foul air. Slowly, her strength returns.

She rises, moves toward the song, the radiance,
the mercy. Finally knows that light trumps darkness
every time. Finds the rusted door sprung wide.

Opening Prison Doors

The bright pink balloon sailed into a powder blue sky, growing smaller and smaller until it disappeared into the heavens. Six of us stood watching, weeping as we sang, "Amazing grace, how sweet the sound, that saved a wretch like me ..."

When Trisha first began post-abortion recovery sessions, she was depressed and often cried. She battled anger and despair, struggling to forgive herself. She suffered from frequent panic attacks. God revealed to Trisha how her anger toward her husband, despair about the future, and anxiety about her job were all tied to the abortion. Once she understood that connection and learned to forgive herself, she felt like a new person.

I saw her not long after we held a memorial for her child. Trisha's countenance had transformed from sad and anxious to radiant and joyful. She couldn't wait to see how God would use her healing to help other women.

Isaiah 61 is a well-loved chapter describing the ministry of the hoped-for Messiah. When Jesus completed his earthly ministry, he handed over the responsibilities of his kingdom to his followers. Now we are his hands and feet and voice. We walk into dungeons with a ring of keys in our hand. We minister freedom to spiritual and emotional captives, including those wounded by abortion.

Remember Nathaniel Hawthorne's *The Scarlet Letter*? Today's scarlet A stands for abortion. A woman branded with this A may have been in an emotional dungeon so long she can't connect the dots anymore. She doesn't know why she's depressed, anxious, and disconnected. A post-abortive man may not realize why he avoids "good" men, has trouble connecting with his family, keeps changing jobs, or struggles with feelings of unworthiness. These hearts drag heavy chains.

Then one day someone shows them the way out. They blink in the brightness of newfound freedom, finally breathing clean air, no longer a captive—instead, a trophy of God's grace.

With a sense of humility and honor, we come alongside those trapped by shame and watch them take hold of God's undeserved favor. Walking beside someone on this journey is another kind of sacred moment. As part of the life-affirming movement, you could be one who unlocks prison doors with the keys Jesus gives you.

"The Spirit of the Lord God is upon me, because the Lord has anointed me to bring good news to the poor; he has sent me to bind up the brokenhearted, to proclaim liberty to the captives, and the opening of the prison to those who are bound..." **—Isaiah 61:1**

Going Deeper

Read all of Isaiah 61 aloud. Picture yourself in the scene. Are you the prisoner, still seeking release from old tormentors? If so, ask God to direct you to a trustworthy person you can share this with. Confession and prayer will bring healing.

Perhaps you see yourself as God's representative, carrying keys and looking for prisoners to release. If so, ask God to set up some divine appointments with captives.

AND HEALING BEGINS

She marks "Christian" under
"Religious Affiliation"; she believes
in God, goes to church off and on.
Does she want a future with the father
of the baby? She rolls her eyes.

He's way too immature. I guess we're just …
sex buddies.

This is her ninth partner. She knows
what God says on the subject.
It doesn't add up until I ask,
Were you ever sexually abused?

She grows quiet. **I was just a kid.**

And there it is, the splintering.
Heart and mind divided, repeating
senseless acts in futile hope for better
outcomes. She lets me pray for her,
says she'll come to church.

I don't believe her. Still,

eight months later she is there, babe
in arms, lifting praises heavenward,
fractured soul bathed in the presence
of the One who makes

all things new.

Growing in Ministry

If you're like me, you love the local church. You're involved in various ministries there. You may wonder, *Can I still serve wholeheartedly at church as I get involved in this ministry to the community?*

The answer is, absolutely. In fact, you'll have more to offer than ever.

When you spend time ministering outside the four walls of the church, God expands the tent pegs of your heart. Your capacity enlarges. Your sensitivity and skill in ministry increase. Your prayer life expands and grows as you pray for the women in crisis you're privileged to help.

You know the joy of working shoulder to shoulder with Christians from other denominations. You learn from them, and they learn from you. Walls come down and bridges are built.

Hours of training hone your skills in counseling. Open-ended questions become second nature, and this helps people open up to you easily. You become more careful about keeping confidences.

You learn some counterintuitive skills, such as asking a young woman for permission to hug her. You understand this is part of respecting her and ensuring she has a voice.

You're better equipped as a homeland missionary to reach out to a post-Christian, postmodern culture. The language of the Millennial generation is no longer foreign, and you've grown more comfortable with helping those caught in generational poverty.

You can articulate what sexual promiscuity does to the brain chemistry of a young woman or young man, and you've seen firsthand the Millennial's confusion and pain regarding the place of sexual expression. You understand how radically our morals have changed in the last few decades.

Solid training helps you share the gospel confidently, perhaps even with those who've never heard of the resurrection of Jesus. It's quite possible you'll introduce a young woman to Jesus. She may even become part of a local church as a result of her visit with you. There, she'll have a spiritual family to help her grow and learn to minister to others—and the cycle of transformation will continue.

One day, a friend at church may pull you aside and say that one of the young women you invited to church was baptized that week.

Now that's what I call a good day at the office. I pray you have many.

"And say to Archippus, 'See that you fulfill the ministry that you have received in the Lord.'" —**Colossians 4:17**

Going Deeper

Put yourself in Archippus' place. Ask God to show you how he wants to increase your effectiveness in ministry through your involvement in life-affirming work. Give him thanks for what he has already done in you.

_____

_____

_____

_____

_____

_____

_____

_____

_____

_____

_____

_____

_____

PSALM 133 EXPANDED

Like costly, fragrant oil is unity,
sweet perfume rising up to heaven's throne;
like dew adorning mountain's majesty.

Oh, how our gracious Father smiles to see
a deep abiding love among his own;
like costly, fragrant oil is unity.

Our service done in true humility
shines like a glittering strand of precious stones;
like dew adorning mountain's majesty.

Of greater worth than fame or royalty
is doing life together in the Son;
like costly, fragrant oil is unity.

The purest song, the richest harmony
brothers compose by joining hearts as one;
like dew adorning mountain's majesty.

How pleasant to be part of God's family,
the ones commanded blessing rests upon;
like costly, fragrant oil is unity;
like dew adorning mountain's majesty.

United We Stand

The air was charged with joy and excitement at the conference. Over 1,300 PRC staff, volunteers, and board members filled the hotel ballroom. Men, women, Asian, Caucasian, African-American, Baptist, Charismatic, Catholic—we all lifted our voices to worship Jesus.

The love in the room was palpable. As we settled down to hear the evening's speaker, she asked us this rhetorical question: "If Planned Parenthood holds conferences, what songs do you suppose they sing?"

There's only one reason people from diverse backgrounds love each other, work together, and rejoice with one another the way Christians do—we all belong to Jesus and he belongs to us. The common ground for all followers of Christ is the foot of his cross.

One thing I've enjoyed most about working in the life-affirming movement is the diversity of backgrounds represented. Many "flavors" of Christians care deeply about protecting the unborn, which provides ample opportunities for two outcomes: we can bicker about doctrinal differences and let them divide us, or we can create the lovely fragrance of unity in the bond of peace, for the sake of Jesus.

As an old friend of mine puts it, no one has the corner on the glory.

My Catholic friends have taught me the importance of using tangible symbols in connecting to Jesus. I attended a weekend workshop by Dr. Theresa Burke, founder of Rachel's Vineyard. She led us through a living Scripture exercise that touched me deeply. I felt as though I were walking in Palestine, one of the multitude listening to Jesus.

My Baptist friends are proficient in their knowledge of Scripture and how to apply it to everyday life. They are good students of the Word, strong in their convictions about applying it to personal sin problems. They also love to share the gospel with boldness, out of a deep concern for people's eternal destiny.

My Charismatic friends emphasize sensitivity to the leading of the Holy Spirit. They seek an intimate relationship with Jesus, listening for his voice throughout the day in many situations.

Every tradition brings something special to the table.

Besides denominational lines, Christians have other differences. There are various personalities, such as introverts and extroverts. There are different age groups, ranging from college-age volunteers to grandmothers teaching classes. There are diverse social classes and ethnic backgrounds.

All these differences provide opportunities for growing in grace. When conflicting issues arise, we can agree to disagree. We can move forward together, refusing to allow our opinions to divide us.

Something powerful happens when Christians lay aside their differences, combine their strengths, and walk humbly with God together.

Something that diffuses the fragrance of heaven.

*"There is one body and one Spirit—just as you were called to the one hope that belongs to your call— one Lord, one faith, one baptism, one God and Father of all, who is over all and through all and in all." —**Ephesians 4:4-6***

Going Deeper

Make two lists, one of doctrinal differences that you see as non-negotiables and one of preferences that aren't deal-breakers when it comes to fellowship. How can these lists help you avoid majoring on minor differences among Christians?

_____

_____

_____

_____

_____

_____

_____

_____

_____

_____

_____

UPSIDE DOWN

In the kingdom of heaven,
where night has dawned to day;
the weak are filled with power,
and the blind lead the way.

Our heartache turns to laughter,
and the lame win the race;
the broken pour the ointment,
and shame is washed by grace.

The wounded are the healers,
and the humble shall be first;
the living water's flowing,
and no one suffers thirst.

Our trials turn to treasure,
and the hungry eat their fill;
the poor possess the riches,
and the storm at last is still.

This kingdom reigns within us,
the sweet taste of life to come;
all our brokenness restored
by the rule of God's own Son.

Let's serve him with our whole heart,
knowing he makes all things new;
Let's daily lay our lives down
for our God, faithful and true.

Who Gets to Be Jesus?

Just days after the passing of his teenage daughter, R.C. Sproul Jr.,
spoke at a pregnancy center conference I attended.[15] All her life, he explained, Shannon's multiple physical challenges needed continual caregiv-
ing for even the most basic needs.

Shannon never listed her needs or complaints, Dr. Sproul said. She
simply allowed her dad to serve her, and he felt privileged to do so. In
describing their relationship, he drew a parallel to life-affirming ministry.

We love to see ourselves as the hands and feet of Jesus to others,
he explained. That's satisfying. But instead, it's those we serve who
represent Christ.

When we minister to others, we minister to Jesus himself. To put
this in terms of life-affirming work, it's not so much about us being Jesus
to the abortion-vulnerable woman. It's about her being Jesus to us.

That's a much more humble position, isn't it? We're the needy ones.
We're widows and orphans, every one.

Remembering that those I serve allow me to do so helps me to hon-
or each person's uniqueness. It keeps me from treating people as com-
modities. The temptation to collect ministry trophies is always a danger,
whether it's notches on our evangelist belt or the number of distressed
pregnant women we've helped.

Jesus has no interest in a ministry machine that produces results. He
always sees the individual and cares about him or her personally.

This truth brings us full circle. If we're truly life affirming, we'll hon-
or, value, and cherish every human life, regardless of his or her challenges,
demeanor, or history. We'll treat everyone with sensitivity and grace.

In the latter days of his life, Henri Nouwen left his writing and
speaking career to take care of a severely disabled man. He found more
meaning in this sacrificial, private service than in having a well-known
Christian voice. In making that commitment, Nouwen's quiet action
shouts to the rest of us.

The broken ones we reach out to wear the countenance of Christ.
When we touch their lives, we minister to Jesus. We often receive thanks

from those we serve—but really, we should be thanking them.

"And the King [Jesus] will answer them, 'Truly, I say to you, as you did it to one of the least of these my brothers, you did it to me.'" —**Matthew 25:40**

Going Deeper

God's kingdom has been described as an upside-down kingdom. In the age to come, we may be surprised by who's highly esteemed in heaven.

Think of a recent time when you served as Jesus' hands and feet by helping someone. Now picture yourself in that same scenario, only you're ministering to Jesus rather than ministering for him. How does that feel different? Does it feel less noble, or does it seem to be more of a privilege?

_____

_____

_____

_____

_____

_____

_____

_____

_____

_____

_____

_____

THE PREACHER'S DREAM

*There are hundreds of them in an
endless single-file line, each
with pile of stubbled straw
and kindling at their feet. Far
away, a Man walks down the line,
regal, hair like snowy wool,
blazing torch in hand. He halts
in front of one man's pile, touches
flame to straw, igniting bright surge;
only embers remain. He moves
to the next pile, lowers the torch.
Flames lick hay, this time leaving
sheen of gold. The Man keeps
walking, the fire testing, revealing.
He is close to the preacher now,
stops by the little blue-haired
lady who taught him Sunday school.
Whoosh. Blaze swallows kindling;
light dances on diamonds, emeralds,
rubies, her favorites, piled waist-high.
Astonished, she weeps, laughs, praises.
The Man moves to the preacher,
fire catches dry grass, and
the preacher, startled, awakes.*

Heavenly Incentives

No good deed done by a believer will go unrewarded by God.

Years ago, a church we attended had a large building that families took turns cleaning. One week, when it was our turn, my husband and I couldn't make it.

Our three teenage sons came to the rescue and thoroughly cleaned the entire building by themselves, without being asked. We wanted to quickly reward such excellent behavior, so we took the boys on a road trip to a hot spring the next day. The weather was so cold they made ice-sculptures with their hair, which amused us all.

The pleasure we felt that day was a small taste of what our heavenly Father looks forward to when he rewards us for our good works.

Paul writes in 1 Corinthians 3:12-14: "Now if anyone builds on the foundation with gold, silver, precious stones, wood, hay, straw—each one's work will become manifest, for the Day will disclose it, because it will be revealed by fire, and the fire will test what sort of work each one has done. If the work that anyone has built on the foundation survives, he will receive a reward."

Life-affirming work isn't glamorous. The general public is much more likely to appreciate other demonstrations of compassion and justice. The little ones we defend may never be able to thank us, but God is especially pleased when we protect the most vulnerable people group on the planet.

We tend to forget how strongly God feels about things—he gets angry, he rejoices, he feels jealous. How deeply he grieves when yet another little one is destroyed, and how his heart sings when one is rescued from the slaughter.

Picture the Lord's smile when he tells you face-to-face, "As you did it to one of the least of these my brothers, you did it to me." Imagine how eager he is to reward you.

Even employers offer incentives as motivation for excellent job performance to help employees care about how well they're doing. Specific rewards are a way for a boss to say, "How well you do your job matters to me."

God knows our hearts. He knows we need rewards to look forward to after the long, hard labors of this life. And he counts many moments of obedience we wouldn't remember.

For years, my husband and I sponsored a child through Compassion International. One evening, I struggled to write a letter to our little girl in Ecuador. I was exhausted, and the letter felt like one more to-do on a lengthy list. Still, I berated myself for not writing lengthier, more frequent letters.

Do you think I don't see the effort you put in? Do you think this doesn't count in my eyes?

The God of all grace surprised me with his gentle reminder. I relaxed, laid my self-imposed burden down, and smiled at the thought of what lay ahead for me.

Have you contemplated your heavenly reward? Or do you find yourself thinking you ought to serve God out of obedience, expecting nothing from him?

"I [Jesus] am coming soon. Hold fast what you have, so that no one may seize your crown." —**Revelation 3:11**

Going Deeper

Read the following passages: 1 Corinthians 9:25, 2 Timothy 4:8, James 1:12, 1 Peter 5:4, and Revelation 2:10 and 3:11. What are the five crowns Christians can receive in the age to come? How does knowing about these crowns affect you?

_____

_____

_____

_____

_____

_____

_____

_____

_____

_____

_____

_____

_____

THE KNOWING

If at times
a playful smile emerges
on my countenance,
and my step quickens
to childhood's skip,
it's because I know secrets
hidden from the beginning of time.

And if at times
I weep with wild abandon,
and my cry deepens
to childhood's wail,
it's because I bear the pain
of strangers and lands unseen.

Far from mad, I am
sounder than ever before;
I have seen through the dark glass,
and my soul has been quickened
with one glimpse of the mystery.
I have heard the voice of many waters;
I have breathed a fragrance
sweeter than earth can offer.

I live beyond these fragile boundaries
of time and space,
in far-flung dimensions
you can only grasp
when your own soul is quickened
and you know
and are known.

Pilgrims on Earth

The pregnancy test showed positive. The teenage couple stared at the floor, her face pale, his shoulders shaking with silent sobs. After they accepted prayer and hugs from me, they stood mute for several more minutes and shuffled out the door.

I closed the door to my office softly and slid into my chair. Then I burst into tears and fell to my knees. Only Jesus could rescue this baby. Only Jesus could bring peace and hope to these young parents. And only Jesus was able to stretch the capacity of my heart so wide I wept for the young strangers I met that day.

The reaction was more than my personal emotions. I felt the pain of two hurting teenagers as though it were my own. When we come to Christ and begin to know him intimately, he increases our ability to love. We're more able to care about others. Our default response changes from selfishness to empathy.

We're enlarged.

The Holy Spirit comes to live inside us, and we value what he values, care about what he cares about, feel what he feels. We begin to know in our hearts, not only our heads, that planet Earth isn't our real home. We live as loyal citizens of another realm.

In that other realm, ending the life of an innocent unborn child is against the law. In that realm, the atmosphere is pure compassion. In that realm, a King rules who will one day make all things new. And in that realm, joy inexpressible and filled with glory permeates the atmosphere—far greater joy than I experienced when the frightened teen couple I had wept over chose life for their baby.

One day, we'll fully enjoy that glorious realm; for now, we have work to do in this world. As we labor in the life-affirming movement, we can get caught up with many details and responsibilities of ministry. We can become so task-oriented we forget why we began this journey.

It's about the unborn, yes; but ultimately, it's about Jesus.

The waiting, the training, the time invested, the rejection—they're all worth it so we may know Jesus and be known by him. In that knowing, our joy runs deep. In that knowing, we savor a satisfaction richer and fuller than any fleeting happiness, for our King himself is the greatest treasure of all.

May you know the Lord Jesus more deeply day by day. And may you rejoice in the intimate way he has always known you—from before the moment of your conception.

"For his sake I have suffered the loss of all things and count them as rubbish, in order that I may gain Christ and be found in him … that I may know him, and the power of his resurrection" **—Philippians 3:8-10**

Going Deeper

Think back to the last time you felt the Lord's presence in a tangible way—perhaps in a quiet time of prayer, or a special church meeting, or as you ministered to someone. Let yourself relive that moment and enjoy it again, giving thanks for it. Ask God for more experiences like that.

If you struggle with feeling God's presence in a tangible way, ask him to reveal himself to you more fully. Come to him with quiet expectancy, believing that he is a good Father who loves to spend time with his children. You may want to prayerfully read Matthew 7:7-11.

_____

_____

_____

_____

_____

_____

_____

_____

_____

_____

The Crown: Looking Back

The water has become too deep, too fast, too strong. You can't fight the river anymore. With a quick plea toward heaven, you let go—and to your surprise, an eddy catches you and swirls you gently toward the shore. God's grace buoys you, and you are borne effortlessly to your goal.

You climb onto the beach, a little shaken, but ready to explore new ground.

Hopefully, the last ten days have given you an irresistible taste of the future. You've seen pictures of lives changed by the hope of the gospel and the mission of the life-affirming movement. You've met rescued babies, grateful mothers, brand-new Christians. You've been introduced to women and men whose lives have been healed from abortion by the grace of God, transformed from brokenness to wholeness by the power of the Holy Spirit.

You've witnessed the beauty of the Church united for the common goal of glorifying the name of Jesus. You've tasted the sheer joy of serving him by standing up for his little ones. You've been reminded that God rewards every good work of the believer in eternity and that this world, as we know it, is only temporary.

Most importantly, you've been encouraged to seek to know Jesus more and more.

Afterword

Congratulations! You've crossed the river. You resisted the tug of uncertainty and bravely traversed the currents of change. Now you stand on the shore of new territory, looking back to where you started.

It's been quite a journey, hasn't it?

From here out, you take ground. You're equipped, encouraged, and eager to reach out to your community. You've rolled up your sleeves to co-labor with Jesus, ready to demonstrate his high regard for every human life.

What does that look like for you?

Perhaps you've cleared a half day in your weekly schedule and started volunteering at your local PRC. Maybe your nursing background is God's way of preparing you to become a life-saving sonographer. Perhaps you've responded to God's call to apply for a position on the board. Or you're praying consistently and fervently for the mission.

Maybe you've decided you're the perfect one to serve as your pregnancy center's church representative, letting your congregation know of needs and upcoming events. Maybe God is challenging you to give like you've never given.

Whatever way you choose to serve Jesus in life-affirming ministry, you see things in a fresh way now. God has been speaking to you, and you've changed.

The number forty speaks of testing, transition, and transformation. Jesus fasted forty days; the Israelites spent forty years in the wilderness; human gestation lasts forty weeks. In these last forty days, I pray that you've moved "from glory to glory" in your growing understanding of

God's heart for the least of these.

Thank you so much for letting me journey alongside you. It's been a privilege to grow in courageous compassion together.

God bless you richly,

Susanne

Acknowledgments

It takes a village to write a book, or so I have found, and I'm so very grateful to those who have supported and encouraged me in this endeavor.

Les Stobbe, you are more than an agent. You are a mentor, a friend, and an invaluable resource. Thank you so much for your generous spirit and your wisdom. Janet Chester Bly, you are a treasure. Thank you for taking the time to advise me on this manuscript and for rounding up some patrons for this project. I'm so very grateful for you and for them.

John Ensor, a warm thank-you from the bottom of my heart for taking this fledgling pro-life writer under your wing and making helpful suggestions for this manuscript.

Mary Chapman, thanks for taking time from your busy schedule at Care Net conference to advise me on this manuscript. You are one gracious lady. Thanks to Care Net staff members Dr. Sandy Christianson, Jacob Hall, and Eve Gleason for your help on facts and statistics. Also thanks to Eve and to Vince DiCaro for the privilege of writing guest posts on Care Net's website.

Many thanks to other leaders in the life-affirming movement: Jor-El Godsey, Tom Glessner, Sol Pitchon, Patrick Eades, Kim Triller, and numerous executive directors of pregnancy resource centers who encouraged me by letting me know of your excitement for this book. You guys rock!

Special thanks to Jim Higgins, Chairman of the Board for Life Choices Clinic, and Judy Higgins. I so appreciate how you helped me get to the Mount Hermon Writers Conference, and I'm so thankful for your ongoing support. Thanks to Karla McKarley for inviting me into the justice/mercy ministry of pregnancy resource center work.

I'm grateful for the writers' groups I've been part of: The "Inklings," led by Patti Lee, whose inspired suggestion of a poetry devotional sparked the idea for this book, and the WOW ("Working on Writing") group led by Terri Picone. Many thanks to Patti and Terri, and to Sharon Hosely,

Brooke Vivian, Jodi Maybury, Pam Thorson, Helen Ross, and Bernice Seward for your feedback and your friendship.

A big thank-you to my prayer partners—Marilyn Steingruber, Clare McCracken, Wendy Neal, Jodi Maybury, Jenny Hoffman, Julie Long and Pam Thorson. Thank you for roaring on my behalf when I felt like whimpering and for upholding me and this project in prayer. Pam, thanks for the many late night phone conversations, and the assurance that I'm not the only person crazy enough to do this writer thing. Grace Thorson, thanks for your helpful input as well.

Many thanks to my editor, Denise Loock, for catching my errors, putting on the polish, and making me look good. You have the heart of a teacher, which I appreciate. Thank you to my publisher, the team at Create Space at Amazon, and all their timely support and help. Thanks, Brian Gage, for your artistic expertise on the eye-catching cover and beautiful interior design. You've been a huge blessing.

To my beta readers (Dale Lavely, Jacqueline Wallace, Jayna Coppedge, Chad Gramling, Christine Denova, Kristyn Mogler, Kristi Bothur, Kendra Burrows, Ted Sugges, and Kim Propp), thank you for your labor of love. I needed your eyes and your quick wits on this. Thanks also to Amy Pittman for dedicating precious hours to proofing this manuscript.

Thanks to the prayer team that upholds Scott and me in this life-affirming ministry –pastors Kevin Beeson and Hugh Laybourn as well as Shelleigh Beeson, Lyndal Stoutin, Sherry Stoutin, Clare McCracken, and Ange Movius. Many thanks to the rest of my church family at River City Church for your support and encouragement. I'm grateful to be a part of you.

Wholehearted thanks to my family: Scott, Daniel and Amanda, Samuel and Jameson, and Jedidiah and Rebecca, for listening to my endless ideas and concerns about this book. You are all such a joy to me. I hope one day Reuel, Aviella, Zaccai, Helaina, and my other (future) grandchildren will benefit from their Nana's book and gain a deep passion for life.

Heartfelt thanks to my parents for raising me to love and serve the Lord Jesus. Thank you, Mama and Papa, for faithfully praying for me all my life and for praying daily over this book until it became a reality. I love you very much.

Finally, all thanks and praise to the Lord Jesus Christ for his manifold kindness to me and for allowing me the privilege of writing this book for his honor.

For Further Reading

The Life-Affirming Mission:
 Answering the Call by John Ensor
 Why Prolife? by Randy Alcorn

Helping Those in Poverty:
 What Every Church Member Should Know about Poverty
 by Bill Ehlig and Ruby K. Payne, Ph.D.

Sex, Brain Chemistry, and Relationships:
 Hooked by Dr. Joe McIlhaney Jr., and Dr. Freda Bush
 How to Avoid Falling in Love with a Jerk by John Van Epp, PhD
 Sex and the Soul of a Woman by Dr. Paula Rinehart
 Not Marked: Finding Hope and Healing after Sexual Abuse
 by Mary DeMuth

Abortion Recovery:
 Her Choice to Heal by Synda Masse
 Forgiven and Set Free by Linda Cochrane
 Surrendering the Secret by Pat Layton

Men and Abortion:
 Fatherhood Aborted by Guy Condon and Dave Hazard

Affiliate Websites:
 www.care-net.org
 www.heartbeatinternational.org
 www.nifla.org

About the Author

Susanne Maynes serves as Counseling Director at **Life Choices Clinic,** a pregnancy resource center where she has been on staff for nine years. She is a certified Biblical Counselor with the Board of Christian Profession- al and Pastoral Counselors and holds a Bachelor of Arts degree in Social Science from Bethany University. She is the winner of a number of writers' contests, and her poems have been published in several magazines, includ- ing the literary journal *Talking River.*

Susanne blogs on topics of church and culture, spiritual growth and Christian parenting at ***www.susannemaynes.com***. She speaks at women's retreats and other events, and she teaches a weekend workshop, Passionate Parenting, for churches. She and her husband, Scott, have been married for 33 years and live in Lewiston, Idaho. They have three grown sons, three daughters-in-law, and four grandchildren (so far), who are the delight of her heart. Besides spending time with her family, a few of Susanne's other favor- ite activities include running by the river, hiking, or having tea with friends.

To contact Susanne:
>   ***www.susannemaynes.com***
>   ***https://www.facebook.com/AuthorSusanneMaynes/***
>   ***https://mobile.twitter.com/susannemaynes***

If you enjoyed this book, please tell others about it and consider writ- ing a review at your favorite online bookstore, such as Amazon, or on social media, such as Goodreads.

Also by Susanne

"*God in Whom We Trust,*" (Day 11), written by *Samuel Maynes* and *Susanne Maynes,* is featured on River City Church's album *Break of Day.* You can listen to it here: ***rivercityworship.us***

Also at ***rivercityworship.us***: You can listen to *"All You Really Need"* (music and lyrics written by Susanne Maynes) on the album *Firm Foundation.*

Coming soon: *"Letting Go Lullaby," (Day 18)* a healing song for those who have suffered pregnancy loss. Watch for details at ***www.susannemaynes.com***

Notes Page

Notes

[1] *Induced Abortion in the United States,"* Guttmacher Institute,
https://www.guttmacher.org/fact-sheet/induced-abortion-united-states (accessed December 10, 2016). Also see
http://www.johnstonsarchive.net/policy/abortion/uslifetimeab.html.

[2] John Ensor, *Answering the Call,* (Peabody: Hendrickson Publishers, 2012), 40-41.

[3] Ensor, *Answering the Call,* 57-59.

[4] 2015 Care Net statistics: Among positive test clients assessed as abortion minded but who did not have an ultra-sound, 25% stated they decided to carry to term. Among positive test clients assessed as abortion minded who did have an ultrasound, 49% stated they had decided to carry to term. Statistics provided by Care Net staff member, Jacob Hall. www.care-net.org.

[5] *"Abortion in America,"* Operation Rescue, http://www.operationrescue.org/about-abortion/abortions-in-america/ (accessed December 10,2016) ORRandy Alconr, *Why Prolife? (Sandy: EPM Publishing, 2004), 78.

[6] J.F. Murphy and K. O'Driscoll, *"Therapeutic Abortion: The Medical Argument,"* NCBI Resources, https://www.ncbi.nlm.nih.gov/pubmed/7129852.

[7] *"The State of the Church 2016,"* Barna.com, https://www.barna.com/research/state-church-2016/ (accessed December 10, 2016).

[8] *"The Asch Conformity Experiments,"* About Education.

[9] Pierson, Anne, *"Touching Hearts, Transforming Lives,"* Workshop, Heartbeat International Conference, Charleston, March 27, 2014.

[10] Joe S. McIlhaney, Jr., M.D. and Freda McKissic Bush, M.D., *Hooked,* (Chicago: Northfield Publishing, 2008), 36-39.

[11] *"The Children's Assessment Center,"* http://www.cachouston.org/child-sexual-abuse-facts/ (accessed Dec. 10, 2016).

[12] Cockroft, Martin, *"What You Need to Know About World Religions,"* http://www.christianitytoday.com/iyf/hottopics/defendingyourfaith/what-you-need-to-know-about-world-religions.html?start=1.

[13] Theresa Burke. *"Traumatic Re-enactment"* presented at Healing Through Truth workshop, hosted by Path of Life, a ministry of Life Services, Spokane, Washington, March 5, 2010.

[14] *"How Therapy Can Help: Before and After Abortion,"* GoodTherapy.org, http://www.goodtherapy.org/learn-about-therapy/issues/abortion.

[15] Sproul, R.C. Jr., Keynote Address, Care Net Conference, Nashville, September 2012, Nashville, TN.

More Praise for
Unleashing Your Courageous Compassion

Unleashing Your Courageous Compassion inspires and encourages us to be bold and courageous with loving people. When we start realizing the truth that God has fully equipped us all to lead others, together we can change the world. He has put specific gifts inside you to carry out his perfect plan and purpose for your life, and this book will help you uncover it as you hear God for the next 40 days.

—Amy Ford, *Co-Founder of Embrace Grace,*
*Author of **A Bump in Life***

I found **Unleashing Your Courageous Compassion** easy to read, and I particularly enjoyed Susanne's insightful and piercing poetry. Her writing is tender and compassionate as well as encouraging and motivating—toward those involved in a past or current abortion decision as well as those who may be ambivalent about answering the Lord's call to minister to those very people. The "going deeper" sections encourage personal introspection without overwhelming the reader with theological head-scratchers.

—April Kesterton, *Executive Director,*
Tulare-Kings Right to Life, Visalia, California

Susanne has created a devotional that is both profound and accessible, both challenging and encouraging, both informational and inspirational. Filled with original poetry, Scripture, research, stories, and her own life experiences, you will come away deeply appreciating your own life—and every human life.

—Keith Ferrin, *Speaker and Blogger, Author of*
How to Enjoy Reading Your Bible

Unleashing Your Courageous Compassion is an exceptional interactive devotional work. Because it is specifically created to draw the body of Christ into his life-giving, life-affirming pregnancy center work, this book will challenge your beliefs, enlarge your heart, and bring you to the point of decision: will I be a voice for those destined to destruction? Susanne has taken her experience and woven it skillfully with God's Word to draw us from the pew to the front lines. No longer can we pour money at the problem; we must pour our lives into restoring a culture of life.

—Becky Wood, Executive Director,
ABC Women's Clinic, Dublin, Georgia

Susanne has provided an invaluable resource in *Unleashing Your Courageous Compassion*. It will prove to be a helpful tool for those seeking to minister compassion to those facing a pregnancy decision, especially, but not limited to, those seeking to minister in the context of a pregnancy resource center. The use of poetry, substantive content, and probing application make each chapter an equipping experience just as much as a devotional experience. I look forward to how this resource will be used to further encourage, equip, and empower God's people to compassionately engage those facing difficult pregnancy decisions.

—Rick Hogaboam, Executive Director,
Lifeline Pregnancy Care Center (Nampa, ID),
Lead Pastor, Sovereign Grace Fellowship (Nampa, ID)

Susanne has effectively communicated God's heart and passion for those he desperately wants to rescue in such an amazing way. *Unleashing Your Courageous Compassion* is a poignant, powerful, insightful, captivating, educational, biblical, and challenging call to action. May the Church of Jesus Christ have ears to hear what the Spirit is saying to us, and may we respond for his kingdom and glory.

—Michelle Sullivan, OT Certified PRC
Training Coach, Omaha, Nebraska

Now that I have read all of *Unleashing Your Courageous Compassion*, I will go back and mine it a day at a time over the next 40 days. What a treasure—Susanne has captured the doubts, trials, joys, and blessings of the ministry in a way that opens the heart. Maybe because I have experienced most of the scenarios in this book, I was brought to tears more than once. I would love to get this book into the hands of every volunteer, board member, staff member, and supporter of pregnancy center work. What an encouragement as well as a call to action and perseverance!

—Mona Parish, *Executive Director,*
Pregnancy Resource Center of Northwest Houston

I am very impressed with the content of this devotional. I believe this would be very beneficial to anyone wanting to get involved with the pregnancy center ministry. The situations are the same, no matter the location. We encounter the same visits, the same conversations about abortion, life, and God. This ministry is unique from other ministries, yet within the movement we share common stories, heartbreaks, and yes, victories! For someone new to the pregnancy center movement, this book clearly defines the ministry, the expectations, and, above all, the grace needed to become a volunteer.

—Gigi Bechthold, *Executive Director,*
Life Choices Clinic, Montrose, Colorado

I was amazed at how relevant Susanne's devotional works are to anyone who works at a pregnancy resource center—client advocates, directors, and church liaisons. It was like she was reading my thoughts— or my heart. After reading Day 1, I was drawn in. By Day 36, I was in tears, knowing that someone could put in words the things I hold in my heart. This devotional was not written just for women, but also for men who have a heart for this ministry. I highly recommend these writings to anyone in pro-life ministry, and I will be sure to have a copy of Susanne's book for everyone who comes to work at our center.

—Susan Young, *Former Executive Director,*
Life Choices Pregnancy Center, Sandpoint, Idaho

In her devotional, *Unleashing Your Courageous Compassion*, Susanne sensitively and powerfully reveals the heart of pregnancy clinic ministry. This honest account explores the devastating effects of our culture on young people today and the truthful, compassionate response offered within a pregnancy help clinic. Susanne presents a compelling, candid look at this unique ministry of life and draws the reader through the doors to introduce them to the way God views his precious creation. *Unleashing Your Courageous Compassion* is a must-read for anyone wishing to know more about pregnancy clinic ministry and many of the crucial issues addressed within their walls.

—Nancy Tefft, *Founder and former Executive Director, Open Arms PCC & Real Choices Clinic, Coeur D'Alene, Idaho*

The Lord's call to protect the vulnerable is clear throughout Scripture and applies to all believers. And who is more vulnerable than the unborn? *Unleashing Your Courageous Compassion* will clarify the call, inspire for the cause, and equip for the challenge of changing a culture. Susanne has demonstrated courageous compassion during her years of service. Let us all commit to exhibiting the same as we protect life in our communities and throughout the world.

—Avonte Jackson, *Former Executive Director, Tri-Cities Pregnancy Network*

Unleashing Your Courageous Compassion is a very powerful collection of devotions, challenges, and eye-opening facts that will move the heart of every reader. This is not a book that condemns, judges, or throws arrows; rather, it uses the power of the Scriptures, imagery, and medical facts to create a compelling argument for all who are considering abortion. It is also a wake-up call for those who are passive about this issue. The value of one life to God, especially an unborn life, is brilliantly revealed in these pages. I highly recommend *Unleashing Your Courageous Compassion* as a resource for anyone who wants to be reawakened to the ongoing fight for every precious life.

—Dave Patterson, *Lead Pastor, The Father's House, Vacaville, California*

I cannot think of a better educational devotional to be used by thousands of staff, volunteers, and faithful champions of pregnancy resource centers throughout the country. Susanne Maynes has created a systematic, compelling, and encouraging devotional that can be used for years to come.

Unleashing Your Courageous Compassion supports those in life-affirming ministries to stand firm in their convictions, uphold the sanctity of human life and winsomely fulfill the Great Commission as they serve others in Jesus' name. Susanne uses true stories, poetry, and accurate information to bring to life various issues such as generational poverty, ministering to young fathers, and understanding relativism in order to share the truth in love with those served in pregnancy centers. This is a devotional that I would love to give to all those who minister at the centers I serve.

—Kim Triller, Executive Director of Care Net Pregnancy and Family Services of Puget Sound, Approved Trainer for Care Net National

Unleashing Your Courageous Compassion is very targeted yet Socratic in its approach—creative yet insightful, tactful yet truthful in its message. This devotional approach to the sanctity of human life and the extension of Christian compassion to those who find themselves with an unwanted pregnancy is a tool of the Holy Spirit. I really think this will speak to this generation.

—Raleigh Galgan, Family Ministries Pastor and former Lead Pastor, Valley Church, Vacaville, California

Along with serving in the pastoral ministry for well over 30 years, my wife and I have also been involved with pro-life ministries and have supported the sanctity of human life movement through various venues. This ministry is huge and can have both an eternal and permanent life-changing impact on both women and men. While there is always a need for additional workers in a very ripe field, there is also an ongoing need for tools to aid and guide in this life-saving ministry. I believe Susanne's book will be a most helpful and life-changing tool. It is both practical and biblical, and I am blessed to endorse her work.

—Arlen Tofslie, Associate Pastor, Dry Creek Bible Church, Belgrade, Montana

In an ocean of conflicting voices regarding the sanctity of human life, we can be tempted to become apathetic. Susanne's words awaken you to the truth that every life matters and every voice matters. Don't read *Unleashing Your Courageous Compassion* if you aren't prepared to love more like Jesus.

—Kevin Beeson, *Pastor, River City Church, Lewiston, Idaho*

In *Unleashing Your Courageous Compassion*, Susanne has offered a rich treasure to the Christian community. While others in the pro-life movement have sought to rally the troops for cultural war through salient battle cries, Susanne whispers an invitation to our hearts in the quiet moments of personal devotion: "Walk with Jesus and me in compassionate care for the vulnerable." With poetic flourish and scriptural insight, she guides her readers along a journey toward closeness to God and purposeful, life-changing service.

—Cliff Purcell, *Lead Pastor, First Church of the Nazarene, Lewiston, Idaho*

In a time in which there are many voices demanding our attention and attempting to shape our beliefs, it is refreshing to read from someone whose agenda is to minister healing to broken people. Susanne's writing comes from experience and carries a compassionate touch without compromising the truths found in Scripture. Her illumination of Scripture is a healing balm as well as an invitation to be involved in the lives of people who need a touch from Jesus. As you read this devotional, I pray that you open your heart to receive grace for healing and to be a healer to others.

—Mike Richardson, *Lead Pastor, Valley Christian Center, Lewiston, Idaho*

Because so many years have passed since the earthshaking Roe v. Wade decision, many people have been worn down by the battle. Conviction still remains but is dampened by years of fighting. Now there are voices even within the church that question how valid our arguments are against this tragedy. What is the believer to do? In this book, Susanne reignites the Christian heart for the things that stir that heart of God. Truth permeates the pages: God's Word, the reality of abortion's lure and pain, and many stories of God's grace. Pastors would do well not only to read this for themselves but also to encourage their congregations. This book will encourage some soldiers to persevere, "for they do not labor in vain," and it will move others to enter the fray for the cause of Christ and the sanctity of all life created in his image.

—*John Stroupe, Pastor, Emmanuel Baptist Church, Lewiston, Idaho*

Wholeheartedness, empathy, compassion, sympathy, intuition, perception, insight—Susanne has carefully woven these threads of human feelings into a marvelous tapestry that encompasses the full and wide range of human emotion. Reading ***Unleashing Your Courageous Compassion***, I was torn. On the one hand, I couldn't put the book down; on the other hand, I wanted to savor the passion in its pages. Be prepared to be deeply moved.

—*Jim Higgins, Board Chair, Life Choices Clinic, Lewiston, Idaho*

66760457R00176

Made in the USA
Lexington, KY
23 August 2017